SEVEN SCHOOLS

— An Introduction

This book offers a simple explanation of different systems of yoga as practiced in India, with special emphasis on those which are likely to be more helpful to the Western student. The author points out that the term yoga has two meanings. The first is union with the divine life that pervades the whole universe. The second is a scientifically arranged curriculum of self-training, study and practice. The different schools of yoga have been developed to suit the varying temperaments of people.

Ernest Wood was born in England and educated in the field of science. As a young man he went to India where he spent many years as an educationist, serving as administrator of various schools, colleges and universities, and also as a worker for the world-wide Theosophical Society. He became deeply interested in the Yoga and Vedanta philosophies and has written a number of books on these subjects, as well as on education and psychology. After leaving India he was for some time President and then Dean of the American Academy of Asian Studies, a graduate school in San Francisco.

This book previously appeared in an Indian edition with the title *The Occult Training of the Hindus*. Also in Quest paperbound editions by the same author are two popular works: *Concentration, An Approach to Meditation*; and *The Pinnacle of Indian Thought*.

SEVEN SCHOOLS OF YOGA
— An Introduction

by
ERNEST WOOD

*This book previously appeared in an Indian edition
under the title*

THE OCCULT TRAINING OF THE HINDUS

A QUEST BOOK
Published under a grant from The Kern Foundation

THE THEOSOPHICAL PUBLISHING HOUSE
Wheaton, Ill., U.S.A.
Madras, India / London, England

First published in India, 1931, under the title *The Occult Training of the Hindus*

First U.S. edition (slightly abridged), 1973, published by The Theosophical Publishing House, Wheaton, Illinois, a department of The Theosophical Society in America

Library of Congress Cataloging in Publication Data
Wood, Ernest, 1883-1965.
   Seven Schools of Yoga.
   (A Quest Book)
   First published in 1931 under title: The Occult Training of the Hindus.
   1. Yoga. I. Title
B132.Y6W588 1973   181'.45   72-13120
ISBN: 0-8356-0435-7

Printed in the United States of America

CONTENTS

Chapter 1

THE SEVEN KINDS OF OCCULTISM

Abnormal Phenomena in India

As soon as one speaks in the Western world about occultism in India, the imagination flies to travelers' stories of marvels that they have seen in that country, of occurrences demanding for their explanation faculties of sense, powers of consciousness and facts of nature beyond the common experience of humankind. Regarding these, I could personally relate a number of weird experiences, sprinkled among the events of a great many years spent in that land.

I must mention the "rope trick" first of all, as it is so widely known. A good account of it appeared in the *Chicago Tribune* some years ago, from the pen of two Americans, who were traveling together in Northern India. At the critical moment, when the little boy was to be seen climbing the rope which had unwound itself vertically into the sky, one of them, who was an artist, made a rapid sketch of what he saw, while the other took photographs. Afterwards the photographs showed no rope or boy in the air, but only the conjurer and his boy standing there with their paraphernalia, and the crowd gathered round. The phenomena were undoubtedly due to some form of hallucination which that conjurer was able to impose upon all these people. I have not seen this "trick" myself, but there are occasional reports of its being done. In *Here, There and Everywhere* Lord Frederic Hamilton relates the experience as told to him by Colonel Barnard. When Chief of Police in Calcutta, the Colonel had been invited with a subordinate officer to witness the feat. They saw the rope ascending, the boy climbing, the man after him, and the man returning with a blood-stained sword; but their camera also revealed that these events had not occurred.

I once met an old gentleman who could do marvels with cards. Two Indian friends were with me at the time. He gave to all of us folded slips of paper in which he had written the names of cards in our presence. I was then required to shuffle my cards, spread them about face downwards, and pick one up. On opening the paper, which had been in my pocket, I found written the name of the card picked up. Next I gathered the cards together, passed them on to my friends, who reshuffled them, spread them out, and had the same experience. After this, I asked the old gentleman to give me a new paper, took up the cards and spread them again; but as I picked one up I willed not to have what he had chosen. The result was that the writing on the paper did not agree with the card. When I showed him this, the experimenter was much astonished, but on my telling him that I had willed not to have his card, he said that that was sufficient explanation, because his method was to concentrate on a card, and transmit the thought of it firmly to my subconscious mind, which could know where the required card lay, and could direct my hand to it.

A surprising experience of the power of thought transference possessed by such people occurred to me some time later, when I was sitting one evening with one of the professors on the staff of my college in Sind, and he was showing some tricks with cards. Suddenly I heard a full-bodied voice speaking clearly, as though in the middle of my head. It pronounced only six words: "Five of clubs. Try that experiment." I at once wrote "five of clubs" on a piece of paper, gave it to the professor, and asked him to shuffle and spread out his cards and pick one up. He did so, and it was the five of clubs. To this day my friend thinks that I played a very clever trick upon him, but my own belief is that the old gentleman performed the whole phenomenon at a distance, after speaking to me telepathically.

On another occasion I had a visit in the middle of the night from a man whom I had never seen or even heard of before. He came in what is sometimes called an "astral body," bringing his own light with him, by which I first saw him (through the wall of the room) coming across the field outside, and watched him until he came into the room and spoke to me. He told me who he was, and afterwards I went to his village, some two hundred miles away, and found him there. He had practiced some form of yoga meditation for many years.

Another man whom I visited gave me a fairly full account of my adventures on the journey, which had occupied several days, and still another told me events yet to come in my life, and even in the lives of my brothers in England, nearly all of which have come out as he said. He told me, for instance, that I would marry at a certain age, about seven years later, and that the lady would have a mole exactly in the middle of her neck, a fact which I did not know until some years later, when the days of short hair came in. Another read my thoughts with the greatest ease, and even transferred them to the mind of a third person, who could then describe in detail the picture I had formed in my mind. The above were all educated men, but once I met a poor shoe-maker who told me that on that day I would miss my train (he could tell by the twitching of his arm!) which I did, for the only time, so far, in my life.

Among more external phenomena, one man transferred some of my own writing from a sheet of paper to the palm of my closed hand, after asking me to close my hands and choose that on which it should appear. Another somehow substituted a living scorpion for a coin held firmly in my wife's closed hand. Another stopped and started the beating of his heart at my bidding; he also, having made a wound in his thigh, caused it to bleed and stop bleeding at my bidding, and afterwards healed the wound completely by a mere passing of his hand over it.

The phenomena experienced in meditation are less susceptible of external observation and judgment. One blind man used to relate to me his visions, some of which I had opportunity of testing. Among those which I could not test was his claim to memory of his previous existence on earth, which he said had occurred about eight hundred years before. The same gentleman showed me the production of a heavy shower of rain over a large field.

The Abnormal Not the Real Occult

But now I have to say that such phenomena are not regarded in India as occultism, or really deep and hidden things, but as very superficial phenomena which the average Indian would not trouble to look at, and certainly would not think of cultivating. These people are sufficiently shrewd to observe that such phenomena are of the same class as those of our daily life, though they may be somewhat rare or unusual. Such cheap magic cannot give them what they really want—release from these restricted and painful conditions of existence, and life in some better condition, which they are able to picture in their minds.

Such mental pictures take two forms in India, as elsewhere. Some people want a supremely glorified earth—that is, a delightful heaven in the company of the great *devas* or god-like angels, in splendid cities and countrysides, beautified with delightful roads having no dust, lined with flowering shade trees, peopled by happy men, women and children, and splendid elephants and horses, and bordered by rivers and ponds bearing the graceful forms of brahmani ducks. That such a life may be lived in the case of persons of great merit, for thousands of years, after death, before it is necessary to return to rebirth, is a common belief.

But other people aim higher than this: they wish to "enter into life." They do not want all those glorious heavens, which offer the same kind of forms as those of the present existence, which can never be completely satisfying. Who wants to play a harp for a long time, or even enjoy the sight of those beautiful elephants and horses and ducks, and the company of the blessed immortals? We want the pure eternal Life, beyond the restrictions of time and space, which is the real occult, that which is hidden from those who cannot rise in thought beyond attachment to these limited states of consciousness.

To those who have vision, that *real occult* is more, not less, than any temporal states of being. That is not an abstraction, but all these things are an abstraction from that, as though a father, seeing that his little son wants to play with his watch, should go and buy him a dummy watch. That real occult is to be known to some extent through those best things in consciousness which rise beyond our individual bodily restrictions—the love which recognizes and values the life in others, the thought which can overstep material limits, and the will which can face danger and destruction in the pursuit of a fuller, freer life, and is thus the advertisement of its own immortality or divinity. Though the average Hindu acknowledges that abnormal psychic powers may come as the aspirant pursues his ideal, he does not seek them, and he takes care that they do not lure him aside with their childish seductiveness. He wants the real occult. So occultism is for him the science of Life or the science of the Self.

How clearly this is put in that most widely respected of all Hindu conduct-guiding scriptures, the *Bhagavad Gita*! The teacher, speaking there as an incarnation of divinity, or as one who has conscious unity with the one life in all, which he has therefore found to be himself, teaches his pupil many things, but now and again he declares what is the most occult of all.

In the ninth chapter he says: "Now I will tell you the most occult of all things, intuition combined with knowledge, having known which you will be liberated from all imperfection." And what is it? "By me this whole universe is pervaded. All beings are placed in me, not I in them. As the wind moves in the sky, all beings are existing in me. I emanate this multitude of beings again and again, yet I am not limited by these activities. The mahatmas, having come to my divine nature, worship with unwavering mind, having known the imperishable source of all."*

In the only two places where the teacher mentions the "most occult" (*guhyatama*) the description is similar. In Chapter 15 after a long description of the

---

* *Op. cit.*, ix. 1, 4, 6, 8, 9. Abridged translation.

Self, seated in the hearts of all, he concludes: "Thus I have told you the most occult teaching. Having understood this, the wise man becomes one who has finished his work."† The teacher concludes all his instruction by saying: "Listen again to my last word, most occult of all. With mind intent on me, become my devotee; sacrifice to me; bow to me. I promise you shall come to me, for you are dear."*
For the further import of this teaching, and the training connected with it, I must refer the reader to chapter three of the present book, but I must mention here that to the Hindu, this, not miracles or magic, is the height of occultism, which I would define as the use of the hidden powers in man to discover the hidden reality in the world.

Shri Shankaracharya, reverenced all over India as of superhuman greatness, endorses the same idea. He speaks of the various practices in which some people indulge, thinking them to be means to the supreme goal of life. Among these he mentions the practices of silence and solitude, posture, fixing the gaze on the tip of the nose, control of breath and restraint of the senses, and declares that: "Real silence is knowledge of that Brahman who is beyond the reach of speech; real solitude is that in which there is no beginning, nor middle, nor end, though it is found everywhere; true posture is dwelling upon Brahman in thought; to see the whole universe as the one Brahman is right concentration of the eye; to feel 'I am Brahman' is the true drawing of the

† xv. 20.
* xviii. 64, 65. Abridged translation.

breath, and the refusal of externals is the outbreathing."* And he derides mere tongue-silence, which is "childish," and the foolishness of tormenting the body with unnatural postures, and the nose with abnormal breathing.

All over India there are people who practice meditation for some time during each day, for the purpose of reaching the most occult thing. These are not only the old-style people of the country places, but in thousands of cases modern men who spend their days in government offices or in business of some kind, and amidst their families, but reserve a special hour for that meditation which is to them a delight, and never a task. For example, I once knew in the south of India a college lecturer, who had four great pleasures in his leisure time. One was to play with his little children, who used to roll over him while he reclined; another, to play the vina (a musical instrument) ; the third, to have an occasional game of chess; and the fourth, to meditate, which was to him a pleasure beyond compare.

Hindu Practicality and Optimism

There is in all a vein of practicality which the West scarcely understands. It is often said by Europeans—as white men in general are called in India —that the Hindus are unpractical, and that their religions are pessimistic. The Hindu makes no reply to this, but he thinks, and says to his neighbor, that

---

* Freely abridged from Shankara's *Aparokshanubhuti,* verses 108-120.

the European, looking through the colored glass of his own personality, imagines what he sees to be of that color.

Consider the example of Gautama, called the Buddha. When, as a youth, he came to realize that the world was full of trouble and sorrow, and his sensitive heart made him feel that of others as though it were his own, he did not accept what is usually called the inevitable, and content himself with keeping sorrow as much as possible out of his own life and that of a few people near and dear to him, but he said, "There must be a solution to this problem, and I am going to find it." Year after year he pursued his purpose, traveling, meditating, and practicing yoga, until he reached "insight vast" and "illumination," and made the spiritual discoveries about the nature of life and the purpose of experience that have since brought happiness and progress to enormous numbers of people.

Again, when Shri Shankaracharya realized that the knowlege that comes to us through the senses was not the fact of the matter, he did not assume, as Europeans are apt to do, that error is finally unavoidable, but set to work, and through yoga opened up the deeper powers of his mind, and thus discovered the truth about things. Those two great people, and others who have successfully followed their path, in giving out their knowledge, say that if a man stops waiting for things to happen, and ceases to lean upon external things, and turns his attention deliberately to the real occult, a great change will take place in his consciousness. Just as you may have a tadpole swimming about under water, and then at a certain stage of the proceedings it develops legs, and issues forth to a wider life outside the water, so you have men, still tadpoles, but the time will come when everyone will use the mind no longer merely as a machine to assist in planning material gains, but as an instrument to see the true relation between man and his environment, and thus to enter consciously into the superhuman life that pervades our world.

If the European then says that it does not appear to him that much practical benefit has resulted to mankind from this teaching, the answer is, "Quite so, so far as Europe is concerned. But not so in India, where thousands of people have deliberately practiced yoga and have succeeded. As to social and physical conditions generally, those will everywhere express more or less the average awakening of the people or nation in which they are found."

Next, the European would say that even if all men believed in man's higher possibilities, it seems that but few may expect to reach them, however much they might try, since life is so short, and many are very undeveloped. The answer to that objection is that among the discoveries of truth is the fact that life is not short. The man is the owner of the body, and when one body is worn out, sooner or later he takes another, and generally a better one, and in fact as many as he needs until he has reached human perfection, and does not require this sort of experience any more. How long it will take him to finish depends entirely upon his own will. If he sets himself, like a good student at a school, to do his best, his progress will be rapid; if not, it will be slow.

The Various Kinds of Yoga

Any efforts deliberately directed to this end may be called yoga. The term yoga means two things. The first is union with the divine life that pervades the world—that is, the goal of human life. The second meaning is a scientifically arranged curriculum of self-training, and study and practice directed to that end. In the practice of yoga we can discern what may be called seven schools. These are not antagonistic, but their methods are somewhat different from one another, to suit the varying minds of men. They are:

1. The Raja Yoga of Patanjali.
2. The Karma and Buddhi Yogas of Shri Krishna.
3. The Jnana Yoga of Shri Shankaracharya.
4. Hatha Yoga.
5. Laya Yoga.
6. Bhakti Yoga.
7. Mantra Yoga.

In Chapters 2, 3 and 4 of this book, I have dealt at length with the first three, all of which are often classed under the general term Raja Yoga. It is *raja* or kingly yoga, because in each case the aspirant aims at becoming completely master of himself and his own life through the use of his own will, love and thought, each of which is a distinct power. They are also divine powers, universal in origin, so in using and developing them the man is always entering more fully into the one ever-present life. The Hindu holds most emphatically, with Emerson, that there is no bar or wall in the human soul where God the cause ceases, and man the effect begins.*

There is a great distinction between the yoga practice which cultivates the mind, and lets the organ or body develop itself in a natural way in unconscious response to that cultivation, and that other method which aims merely at the purification and development of the instrument or body, so that the greater powers of life may shine through the form (*a*) either subdued and emaciated, or (*b*) having its latent organs stimulated into activity, as the case may be.

General terms for these two opposite methods are the Raja Yoga or kingly yoga, so-called because the man becomes king or master of his own faculties and propensities, and the Hatha Yoga, so called from a certain portion of its teaching, as to the practice of special methods of dealing with the incoming and outgoing, or *ha* and *tha,* breaths, by which it is intended to affect the instrument, the body, so that it in turn will affect the Self within. Then, while the first three may be grouped together under the heading Raja Yoga, the last four may be classed under the term Hatha Yoga. The distinction between the groups is that the latter proceeds by external methods,

---

* Essay on "The Over-Soul".

which operate on the bodies, while the former proceeds by methods working in consciousness itself. I know that some may think my inclusion of Bhakti Yoga, or devotion, in the latter list to be very unexpected, but I will clearly justify that classification presently, when we arrive at a description and analysis of these schools.

The three Raja Yogas may be practiced up to quite an advanced point without danger (except to fools, to whom everything is dangerous), without the presence of a personal teacher, but merely with the aid of such a book as this. But the other four should not be so practiced, and anyone who takes them up thoroughly does so at the imminent risk of most serious bodily disorder, disease and even madness. I will give some account of them in Chapter 5.

CHAPTER 2

FREEDOM THROUGH WILL — THE FIRST RAJA YOGA

The Method of Yoga

Patanjali, in his famous Yoga Sutras, or aphorisms, describes yoga as *chitta vritti nirodha*.* *Chitta* is the mind, the instrument that stands between the man and the world. As a gardener uses a spade for digging, so a man uses the mind for dealing with the world. Acted upon by the things of the outer world through the senses, it presents to the man within a picture of those things, as on the plate of a camera. Acted upon by the will of the man within, it transmits into action in the body the thought power that is its positive characteristic. It thus has two functions—one receptive or negative, the other active or positive. It transmits from the world to the man within, and also from the man within to the outer world. *Vritti* means a whirlpool, and *nirodha* signifies restraint or control. Thus yoga practice is control of the whirlpools or changes of the mind or, in simple terms, voluntary direction of what is commonly called thought.

* Sutra i. 2.

The mind of the average man is far from being an instrument within his control. It is being impressed at all times, even during sleep to some extent, with the pictures of a thousand objects clamoring for his attention, through ears, skin, eyes, nose and mouth, and by telepathic impressions from others. In addition to all that, it is in a state of agitation on its own account, bubbling in a hundred places with disturbing visions, excited by uncontrolled emotion or worrying thought. Let him achieve control of all this, says Patanjali, and his reward will be that he shall remain in his own state.*

That a man should be in his own true state has two meanings: first, that in his repose he will be utterly himself, not troubled with the whirlpools, which, however slight, are in the eyes of the yogi† nothing but worry, and secondly, that in his activity as a man, using the mind, he will be a positive thinker, not merely a receptacle for impressions from outside and ideas which he has collected in the course of time.

Ideas in the mind should be material for thought, not merely ideas, just as the muscles are useful means of action, not mere lumps of flesh. Yet it must be confessed in many cases that we have spent all our mental energy in grasping some ideas put before us, and have none left for thinking with, that is for employing those ideas in positive mental work. To be a positive thinker, lover and willer, master in one's own house, is to be oneself, in one's own true state;

---

* i. 3.

† A person who practices yoga.

all the rest is slavery or bondage, willing or unwilling.*

The aim of Patanjali's yoga is just this—to achieve
freedom, as men think of God as free. The technical
name for this great achievement is *kaivalya,* independence.† That is really only another name for divinity,
for material things are in bondage, unable to move
of themselves, and, like a billiard ball, always moved
by forces from the outside; but the divine is free,
able to move of itself, and to act upon other beings
and things. Every man feels in himself some spark
of that divine freedom, which he then calls the will,
and that is the power with which he can control his
mind.

I have spoken of Patanjali's yoga as the yoga of
will, the raja or kingly yoga *par excellence,* because
in every part of it, at every stage, the aspirant uses
his will in self-control. Thought governs things, we
know; so much so, in fact, that every voluntary movement of the body follows a mental picture; therefore
all work done by us, even with the hands, is done by
thought power. But will controls thought, concen-
trates it, expands it, checks it, causes its flow, directs,
in fact, the three great operations of concentration,
meditation, and contemplation.

Before embarking upon the systematic description
of the practices of yoga, which begins in his second
book, Patanjali mentions two things which are neces-

---

* "To its master, the man, the *vrittis* of *chitta* are always only
objects of knowledge, because of his not being involved in them.
The mind is not self-illuminating, because it is objective, and
both mind and man cannot be cognized by the same act." iv. 18-20.

† iv. 34, 26, iii. 54, 49.

sary for success in controlling the *vrittis,* namely
abhyasa and *vairagya. Abhyasa* means constant practice in the effort to secure steadiness of mind,* and
vairagya is that condition of the feelings in which
they are not colored by outside things, but are directed
only by our own best judgment.† This detachment
of the emotions may be lower *(apara-vairagya)* or
higher *(para-vairagya)*, according as it is born from
dislike of external conditions, or from a vision of
the glorious joy of the pure free life.‡ Obviously,
in these two methods we have the will at work, controlling the flow of both thought and emotion.

After declaring that the higher *vairagya* leads to
the highest contemplation, and therefore to freedom,
Patanjali gives the enquirer a foretaste of what is
necessary in the way of meditation and self-purifica-
tion before the higher contemplation leading to freedom is attained, but I need not now deal with those
sutras, as their purport appears again in the systematic course which I will describe.

The Kriya Yoga

When we come to consider Patanjali's systematic
instruction for practical training for yoga, which occupies about one half of his nearly two hundred
aphorisms, we find that it is given in two portions.
The first part, called *Kriya Yoga,*§ is often translated "preliminary yoga." It is that, for if a person

* i. 13.
† i. 15.
‡ i. 16.
§ ii. 1 *et seq.*

has not first practiced it he is not likely to succeed in the second portion, the *ashtanga‡*, or "eight limbs" of yoga practice. But it is much more than preliminary. It is the yoga of action, the yoga which must be practiced all the time in daily life. Without it, meditation would be useless, for yoga is not an artificial attainment, the opening of a door into another life, but a great change in attitude toward oneself and the world. Right in the thick of life's activities our freedom must be realized, for to desire to slip away into some untroubled sphere would be to deny the possibility of our real freedom. A man must be master of himself, whatever other people and beings, whose activities constitute the major portion of his world, may do.

The Five Afflictions

The object of the yoga of action is to weaken what are called the five *kleshas*. A *klesha* is literally an affliction, just as one would speak of a crooked spine or blindness or cancer as an affliction. The five afflictions are *avidya, asmita, raga, dwesha* and *abhinivesha,* which may be translated ignorance, egotism, liking, disliking and clinging to bodily life.* Every one of these might easily be the subject of a long lecture, or even a book, but I must be content with a

‡ ii. 29 *et seq.*

* ii. 3. The commentator Vyasa calls them the five kinds of wrong knowledge or mistakes (*viparyaya,* or hallucination, as when one mistakes a rope for a snake), and adds that, when active, they bring one under the authority of nature, and produce instability, a stream of causes and effects in the world, and dependence upon others.

few words about each. They are faults of the man himself, not outside causes of trouble; the world can never hurt us, except through our own faults, and these five reduce us to pitiful slavery.

Ignorance might be better called unwisdom, for it applies to all those activities of the mind which do not take into account the fact that man is eternal, pure and painless.* Since all objects are known as of a certain nature and character only in relation to a knower, it is clear that the man who does not know his own true nature as eternal, pure and painless, will know no object properly. A house, a chair and a pen are something to a man by which he can satisfy his body and mind, which require protection from the weather, rest and expression in writing. They could not be the same things to an elephant. But the question now is: what are all these things to the real man, who is eternal, pure and painless? To look at all things as for the use of such a being is to begin to see them without error.

Egotism is the tendency to think "I am this,"† and the desire that other people should also think one to be this or that. But the proper form of thought of self is "I am the willer, the lover, the thinker, using the body as an instrument for the expression and development of these powers." Thinking oneself to be a thing, even though it be an excellent and useful personality, means attachment to things. It gives rise to every sort of greed, a potent cause of sorrow and pain, which are always an indication of some-

* ii. 5.
† ii. 6.

thing wrong, not with the world, but with ourselves.

Liking and *disliking* are those unreasoning impulses which lead us to judge and value things by their influence on the comforts and pleasures of the personality, not according to their value for an immortal being.† It is characteristic of the thoroughness of the East that men believing in their immortality apply the idea to their present life, and do not act as though mortal till they die, thinking afterwards to put on an immortality that does not concern their earthly condition.

Clinging to the body indicates the lack of that insight which causes a man to regard the body as a mere instrument, which he is willing to use, and wear out in the course of time.* Many are afraid of the simplest adventure, because the body might suffer. They are like a man of whom I heard, who bought a new motor car, and used to go and sit in it in his garage to enjoy his new possession, but could not bring himself to run it out on the road, lest its newness should be lost, or perchance it should meet with some mishap.

In this affliction we have not merely the fear of death, but that of old age as well, for men forget that the bodily life has its phases—childhood, youth, manhood and old age—and each of these has its own perfections, though it has not the perfections of the other stages. There is constant apparent loss as well as gain, because no man can pay attention to all the lessons of life at once, or exert at the same

† ii. 7, 8.
* ii. 9.

time all his faculties, any more than a child in school can properly think of geography, history, and mathematics in the period which is devoted to music.

In Hindu life, before it was disturbed from the West, men were wise enough in old age to give the family business into the hands of their mature sons, and devote themselves to the study and contemplation of life; and just as in the West it is considered the bounden duty of parents to support their children with every kindness and give them the opportunities that their stage in life requires, so was it always considered in the East the duty of the children to support their elders with every kindness, treat them with honor and dignity as the source of their own opportunity and power, and give them every opportunity that *their* stage of life requires.

Let the would-be yogi, then, fix his eye on the long life of the soul, which uses many bodies, one after another, and advances on the path to the perfection of character that is freedom by keeping its goal ever in view.

Removal of the Afflictions

It is not presumed that in the preliminary stage the candidate will destroy these *kleshas*. His object will be attained if he succeeds in definitely weakening them. Three kinds of practices are prescribed for this purpose in the yoga of action. These are called *tapas, swadhyaya,* and *ishwara-pranidhana.**

It is impossible to translate these terms by a sin-

---
* ii. 1.

gle word each, without causing the most serious mis-understanding. The first is often called austerity, and I have seen it described even as mortification. The word means literally "heat," and the nearest English equivalent to that when it is applied to human conduct is "effort." The yogi must definitely do those things that are good, even when a special effort is necessary because old habits of the personality stand in the way. Briefly it means this: "Do for the body what you know to be good for it, disregarding mere comfort. Do not let laziness, selfishness, or indifference stand in the way of your doing what you can to make your personality healthy and efficient in the work that it ought to be doing in the world."

Patanjali does not explain the practice of *tapas,* but Shri Krishna says, in the seventeenth chapter of the *Bhagavad Gita*: "Reverence to the gods, the educated, the teachers and the wise, purity, straightforwardness, continence, and harmlessness are the *tapas* of the body; speech truthful, pleasant and beneficial, and study of the sacred words are the *tapas* of speech; cheerfulness, balance, silence, self-control, and being true to oneself are the *tapas* of mind."* How then can anyone say that *tapas* is self-torture? It is true that there has grown up a system of painful practices, such as that of holding the arm still until it withers, or sitting in the sun in the midst of a ring of fires, but these are superstitions which have grown up round a valuable thing, as they are liable to do everywhere. Those who follow these methods are

---

* xvii. 14, 16.

few as compared with the true yogis. All over the country there are Indian gentlemen—many of them government servants who have a routine task with short working hours—who every day spend some time in meditation, deliberately guiding themselves by the Yoga Sutras.

The second practice, *swadhyaya,* means the study of books that really concern yourself as an immortal being. Give up indiscriminate reading, and study what bears upon your progress.

The third practice, *ishwara-pranidhana,* means devotion to God,* but to God as understood by the Hindu, as the perfect Man pervading all things, the life of the world, the great consciousness of which that of each one of us is but a share, just as the body is a share of the matter of the world. The aspirant must habituate himself to see that in everything, to accept all as from that hand. "Everything that is received is a gift," says a Hindu proverb; more than that, it is a gift from God, presented with perfect wisdom, to be accepted, therefore, with the greatest cheerfulness and joy. Behind the eyes of every person he meets, the aspirant must also see the divine. The common salutation of the Hindu, with the palms together, looks curious to the European, as resembling prayer. It is prayer—the recognition of God in our fellow-man.

This practice develops right emotion; the previous one right thought; and the first, right use of the will

---

* Patanjali's idea of God is given in the Sutras, i. 24-26. "God is a superior soul, unaffected by troubles or actions, the source of all knowledge, unlimited by time." Abridged translation.

in work; and the three together, pursued diligently for a time, play havoc with the five afflictions.

When the candidate has weakened the afflictions to some extent, he is ready for the eight great "limbs" of yoga. These may be divided into three sets: two moral, three external, and three internal.

The Two Moral Limbs of Yoga

The two moral "limbs" of yoga contain five rules each, which the man must practice in his daily life. Put together, they make what we may call "the ten commandments." The first five are: "Thou shalt not (a) injure, (b) lie, (c) steal, (d) be incontinent, and (e) be greedy."*

Explaining this aphorism, Vyasa says that *ahimsa* or non-injury is placed first because it is the source of the following nine. Thus the brotherhood principle is considered as fundamental. Only he who is in that relation with other beings can follow up the practice of yoga with any hope of success. Truth, for example, can hardly arise unless there is a motive beyond selfish desires. Vyasa explains that it means word and thought being in accordance with facts to the best of our knowledge. Only if speech is not deceptive, confused or empty of knowledge, he says, is it truth, because speech is uttered for the purpose of transferring one's knowledge to another.

Vachaspati's gloss interprets truth as word and thought in accordance with facts, and fact as what is really believed or understood by us on account of

---

* ii. 30

our own direct experience, our best judgment or the accepted testimony of others. So yoga is rooted in virtue, and that in brotherhood, or a feeling for others. I have explained it only in terms of truth, but similar reasons can also be given to show that the other virtues—also necessary for yoga—are attainable only to the unselfish. Those virtues are also to be practiced in thought as well as in deed, for they are to be not merely restraints, but changes in the character, implying inward purity and strength. Without the inward desire for them, the practice would be very false.

The second five are: "Thou shalt be (a) clean, (b) content, (c) self-controlled, (d) studious, and (e) devoted."* Few comments are needed on these. Contentment does not mean satisfaction, but willingness to accept things as they are and to make the most of them. Without dissatisfaction one would not take to yoga. It implies a desire to improve one's life. The remaining three are *tapas, swadhyaya,* and *ishwara-pranidhana* appearing once more. It is by dwelling upon them that all these virtues are to be attained. Patanjali explains that when thoughts of sins arise they should be immediately and deliberately replaced by thoughts of these virtues.†

Incidentally, Patanjali mentions that when the ten virtues are firmly established in a person's character there are definite effects in the environment as well as in the mind, such as absence of danger, effectiveness of speech, the arrival of unsought wealth, vigor

---

* ii. 32.
† ii. 33, 34.

of body and mind, understanding of life's events, clarity of thought, steadiness of attention, control of the senses, great happiness, perfection of body and senses, intuition, and realization of one's true self.*

The Three External Limbs of Yoga

Now we come to what some will regard as the more practical steps, though to the Hindu nothing can be more practical than the ten commandments. Of these the three external steps are *asana, pranayama,* and *pratyahara.* The first is right posture, the second right breathing, and the third control of the senses. They mean the control of the outer instrument or body, so that it will offer no impediment to the serious practices of meditation which are to follow.

First, one must learn to sit quite still in any healthy position. "The posture must be steady and pleasant,"† says Patanjali—that is all. There is no recommendation of any particular posture, least of all any distorted, painful, or unhealthy position. Posture is achieved when it becomes effortless and the mind easily forgets the body.

Next, regulation of breath is necessary, control of the points at which inbreathing and outbreathing should stop and begin again.‡ During meditation, people often forget to breathe normally: sometimes they breathe out and forget to breathe in again, and

* ii. 35-45.
† ii. 46.
‡ ii. 49.

so are suddenly recalled to earth by the choking of the body. Indeed many people never breathe well and regularly at all; let them practice simple natural exercises, such as those recommended by teachers of singing, and take care that the body is breathing regularly before they enter their meditation.

Sometimes numbers or proportionate times are prescribed, and one of the most authoritative in India is that in which one breathes in with the number 1, holds the breath with the number 4, breathes out with the number 2, and immediately begins again; but it is impossible to prescribe the perfect numbers, because they must differ with different people, or to say whether such a large proportion of retention is good. The question is: how long must you retain the air that you have taken into the lungs, so as to provide of its complete oxidation? Science will some day say. But you must not hold it in longer than that, for to do so is equivalent to breathing nitrogen, water vapor, and carbonic acid gas, with no oxygen at all. Better too short than too long, for, in the former case, though the muscles may overwork, the brain will be properly supplied with aerated blood.

The only practical advice one can give is that the breathing should be regular and a little slow, and there should be a short pause between inbreathing and outbreathing. It should also be calm, as may be judged by its not causing much disturbance in the outside air. Stunts such as breathing up one nostril and down the other, or holding the breath for a long time, have no place in Patanjali's system, and should generally be avoided as dangerous.

Pratyahara is the holding back of the senses from the objects of sense.* One must practice paying no attention to sounds or sights or skin sensations, so that they will create no disturbance during meditation.

Think of what happens when you are reading an interesting book. Some one may come into the room where you are, may walk past you to get something, and go out again; but perhaps you heard and saw nothing at all. You were in what is sometimes called a brown study. Your ears were open and the waves of sound in the air were no doubt agitating the tympanum, from which the nerves were carrying their message to the brain. Your eyes were open, and the light waves were painting their pictures on the retina, but you saw and heard nothing, because your attention was turned away from those sensations.

The yogi must try to do all that at will, so that in his meditation no external sight or sound will distract him. This means also a considerable control of the emotions, that he may have no curiosity whatever about anything in the world during the time that he has set apart for his meditation. One way of practicing this is to sit and listen for a while to the various sounds of nature; then listen to the delicate sound in the ear and so forget the former (though you cannot watch yourself forgetting it) ; then listen to a mere mental sound conjured up by the imagination, and so forget even the music in the ear.

---

* ii. 54.

The Three Internal Limbs

Then come the three internal steps, to which everything else has been leading up, called *dharana, dhyana,* and *samadhi*. They are concentration, meditation, and contemplation.

Concentration is the narrowing of the field of attention, the fixing of the mental eye upon a chosen object.* If you practice concentration or meditation, always choose the object before you begin. Sometimes people sit down and then try to decide what to concentrate upon, and come to no definite decision before all their time is gone. Then, do not try to hold the object in position by your thought. It is not the object that is going to run away; it is the mind that wanders. Let the object be thought of as in a natural position—if it is a pen it may be lying on the table; if it is a picture it may be hanging on the wall. Then narrow the field of attention down to it, and look at it with perfect calmness, and without any strain or sensation in the body or head.

Do not be surprised or annoyed if other thoughts intrude on your concentration. Be satisfied if you do not lose sight of your chosen object, if it remains the central thing before your attention. Take no notice of the intruding thoughts. Say, "I do not care whether they are there or not." Keep the emotions calm in this manner, and the intruders will bow themselves out when you are not looking. Utter calmness—no physical strain, no emotional strain, no mental strain—is necessary for successful concentra-

---

* iii. 1.

tion, and, given this, it is not at all the difficult thing that it is sometimes supposed to be.

Meditation is a regular flow of thought with regard to the object of your concentration.* It is the realization of that object as fully as possible. But you must not let the string of thought go so far away on any line that the central object is in any way dimmed. On the contrary, every new thought that you bring forward with reference to it should make it clearer and stronger than before. Thus you might meditate on a cat. You would consider it in every detail; think of all its parts and qualities, physical, emotional, mental, moral and spiritual; think of its relation to other animals, and of particular cats that you have known. When this is done you should know what a cat is much better than you ever did before.

The same method applies to virtues: truth, kindness, courage. Many people have the most imperfect ideas as to what these are. Make concrete pictures in the imagination of acts of kindness, courage, truth. Then try to realize the states of emotion and mind, and the moral condition, that lie behind them, and in doing so carry upwards the vividness of consciousness that has already been attained in the beginning of the practice on account of concentration on the concrete scene.

In meditation you take something up, but it is the opposite of going to sleep, because you retain the vivid qualities of reality and rationality which belong ·to the world of the senses in the waking state.

---

* iii. 2.

Yet it should always be done with perfect calm, and no exhibition of force.

Contemplation is another kind of concentration; this time at the top end of your line of thought.* When in meditation you have reached the highest and fullest thought you can about the chosen object, and your mind begins to waver, do not try to go forward, but do not go backward. Hold what you have attained, and concentrate calmly on it for a little time. Afterwards drop the meditation, and begin again, then or at another time.

You will find that by contemplation you have created a platform. You have been focusing the awakened creative power of the higher self upon an up-till-now undeveloped portion of your psychic anatomy. But always remember that there is to be no strain; otherwise the practice may injure the brain. If there is no strain it is perfectly safe. Then contemplation opens the door of the mind to intuitive knowledge, and many powers.

The word *sanyama* is used to indicate the triple process of concentration, meditation and contemplation, as applied to any object.†

If the candidate wants to have what are commonly called psychic faculties and powers, Patanjali explains how he may obtain them—by *sanyama* on various objects having corresponding qualities. He mentions knowledge of past and future, memory of past lives, reading of others' minds, perception of those who have reached perfection, and other powers

---

* iii. 3.

† iii. 4.

and knowledge connected with "higher hearing, touch, sight, taste and smell,"† but remarks that, though these are accomplishments of the outgoing mind, they are obstacles to full *samadhi*.‡ Vachaspati, in his gloss, adds that sometimes the mind is captivated by these things, just as a beggar may think of the possession of a little wealth as abundant riches, but the real yogi will reject them all. How can the real man, he asks, who has determined to remove all pain, take pleasure in such accomplishments, which are opposed to his true state of being? Only by non-attachment to all such things, however great, may the seeds of bondage be destroyed, and *kaivalya* be attained.*

Such is the steadfastness of the yogi in pursuit of essential things that he will not permit himself to be detained by these glorious temptations, which can sometimes be so intoxicating to the personality. He is not detained even by such desires as these powers could fulfill, but, filled with the spiritual desires of the higher self, his eye is fixed on the supernal glory of the divine. His aim in treading this path of power is to put an end to the voyages of birth and death, and enter into the glorious freedom and reality of the divine or self-illuminating life.

---

† iii. 35.
‡ iii. 36.
* iii. 49.

CHAPTER 3

UNITY THROUGH FEELING — THE SECOND RAJA YOGA

The Divinity of Man

It is a constant peculiarity of Hindu religious thought that it presumes that the goal of human life, the height of happiness, is to be attained by special effort on the part of human beings. From their point of view nothing much is gained by the mere routine of life. It may continue for hundreds or even thousands of incarnations, punctuated by short or long intervals in heaven. In the course of that experience a man may become more and more capable of seeing his way out of the tangled forest of ordinary life, with its confused and foolish desires, and all the troubles that they generate, and he may discover the height of life itself, which in its purity is free and happy. But only when he sees and wants "the true life kept for him who false puts by," and deliberately aims to make it his own, or to unite himself with that, can he take one step toward freedom, unity and peace.

Sometimes this change has been called a path, but that is only in a secondary sense, for, as an old Mahratta work says, "without moving is the traveling in this road." The man must change himself; that is all. It is not difficult to change ourselves—our own habits of thought and emotion—but it is troublesome, and therefore most people go on wandering in the forest of confused purposes and ideas.

There is one life in which we all have being. Just as the fingers of the hand are rooted in one hand, so that they work in constant relation to one another, whether of antagonism or harmony, so, too, men are rooted in one life. They make the mistake of thinking themselves to be of the earth, and so they become excited, passionate, and quarrelsome about material things. The man who in the midst of all that trouble can preserve a god-like independence and calm is fit for the realization of the one life.

In this Hindu view there is something very much like the outlook of the more practical of the Stoics. Epictetus spoke of reason as the God in man. Seneca put the same thought very clearly: "God is near thee; he is with thee. A high spirit resides within us, the observer of good and evil, and our constant guardian. . . Could anyone rise above the power of fortune without his assistance? It is he that inspires us with thoughts upright, just and pure. . . If you see a man unterrified by danger, untainted with lustful desires, happy in adversity, collected and possessed amidst a storm, looking down as if from an eminence upon man, and on a level with the gods, seems he not a subject of veneration? . . . So great a quality cannot subsist but by the help of God. He is there in part, though still remaining above in the heavens. As the rays of the sun reach, and with their influence pierce the earth, and yet are still above in the body whence they proceeded; so a Mind great and holy . . . dwells indeed with us, but still adheres to its original; it depends upon that; thither tend all its views and endeavors, vastly superior to, however concerned in, human affairs."*

A life utterly true to this godliness of ours is the means to our union with the divine, which may be described as that which is free from all outside interference, which is self-existent and self-illuminating. All manifestation is less than that. Cover up the major portion of reality, and the world of the mere human being is left. This godliness of man is seen in three parts of his being—his will, his love and understanding.

We have studied the use of the will in the previous chapter, and seen how it is applied by Patanjali to man's achievement of perfection and freedom. In the present chapter we will study the way to perfection and unity through love. The book most favored by those who desire above everything else the peace of perfect harmony with all the rest of life is the *Bhagavad Gita,* which contains a conversation between Shri Krishna, commonly regarded by the Hindus as a special direct incarnation of the Divine Life, and one of his followers, Arjuna, a noted soldier.

---

* Ep. 10. (Thos. Morell).

The Test of Fitness

Shri Krishna of the *Bhagavad Gita* was Krishna the King, not Krishna the boy, although he, too, stands as a great awakener of love. That child was a striking figure in the literature of the world, for he so won the hearts of all by his charming pranks that he was hailed as an incarnation of the fount of love which lives at the heart of the world.

Tradition has it that Krishna the King lived five thousand years ago as a great incarnation or *avatara* (descent) of Vishnu, the second member of the divine Trinity, and that he gave his teaching especially to his pupil Arjuna, for whom he acted as charioteer in the war between the Pandavas and the Kurus in northern India.

The way in which that teaching began is full of significance. Before the battle, Shri Krishna drove Arjuna into the space between the two armies, that he might survey their array. Then Arjuna, looking round, was filled with love for the people on both sides, enemies as well as friends, and with horror at the thought of their impending destruction. He sank down in his chariot, and said that he would not fight: "I do not desire victory, or kingship, or pleasures, O Krishna. What is the good of kingship, or enjoyments, or even life to us, O Govinda, when those for whose sake we desire kingship, enjoyments and pleasures stand here ready to fight, throwing away life and wealth. I do not wish to slay them, O Madhusudana, even if myself killed, though it were to gain the kingship of the three worlds."*

That was Arjuna's test. Had he not felt love as the mainspring of his life's interest and activities, it would not have been safe for his teacher to impress upon him very realistically the teaching that he thereupon gave. He said: "You have sorrowed for those who need no sorrow, yet you speak words of wisdom. Those who know do not grieve for the living, nor for the dead. Certainly never at any time was I not, nor you, nor these lords of men, nor shall we ever cease to be hereafter. As there is for the owner of the body childhood, youth and old age in this body, so there comes another body; the intelligent man is not confused by that. Just as a man, having cast off his worn-out clothes, obtains others which are new, so the owner of the body, having thrown away old bodies, goes to new ones. Weapons do not cut him; fire does not burn him; waters do not wet him; the wind does not dry him away. . . Therefore stand up, O son of Kunti, determined to fight."†

This is a glorious truth, but dangerous to the man without love, if it should lead him to be disregardful of the bodies of others in the pursuit of his own ambitions.

Love and Work

But even then, it will be asked, why should not Arjuna, feeling thus, abstain from fighting? For the very simple reason that the man who loves cannot

---

* i. 32, 33, 35.
† ii. 11-13, 22, 23.

abstain from activity. He is in a vigorous state, for love is the great energy of the soul. He is like the typical gentleman of Confucius, who was defined as never neutral, but always impartial.

The man of love looks out upon the world, and feels that he must do what he can, however small the opportunity, for the welfare of mankind. This great fact was also soon placed before Arjuna by his teacher. He pointed out how all the living beings in the world are related to one another in service, how everywhere there is interdependence, and then declared that the man who on earth does not follow the wheel thus revolving lives in vain. Said Shri Krishna, "The man who performs actions without personal attachment reaches the highest; therefore always do work which ought to be done, without personal attachment. Janaka and others attained perfection through work, so, having regard to the welfare of the world, it is proper for you to work."* There is great significance in the words which have been translated "the welfare of the world." They are *loka-sangraha; loka* means the inhabitants; *sangraha* means their gathering together, living in harmony.

It is in this activity that work and love are brought together, and what is called Karma Yoga comes into being. Mere work or karma is not yoga, but when that work is energized by love for mankind it becomes yoga, that is, a method for the realization of the unity of life. So Karma Yoga is one branch of Krishna's great teaching of love. The Karma Yogi "goes about doing good."

---

* iii. 19, 20.

Devotion

And yet that Karma Yoga is also devotion to God.
Among Krishna's devotees, as among those of Christ,
there are two distinct kinds. There are those who
admire the teacher because he was the great lover
of mankind; and there are those who fall down in admiration and devotion before the greatness and goodness of the teacher, and then learn from him to
spread some of his love around them, among their
fellow-men. Some love man first and God afterwards;
others love God first and man afterwards. The first
are the karma yogis; the second the bhakti yogis.

God himself is depicted in the *Bhagavad Gita* as
the greatest karma yogi, the pattern for all who would
follow that path. He says: "There is nothing in the
three worlds, O Partha, that I ought to do, and
nothing attainable unattained, yet I engage in work.
Certainly if I did not always engage in work without
laziness, men on all sides would follow my path.
These worlds would become lost if I did not work;
I should be the maker of confusion, and should ruin
these creatures."* No reason can be given why he
should thus work, except that he loves the world.

But let no man be discouraged because he himself is small. Let not his vision of great things and
devotion to great beings cause him to sink down dis-
consolate, thinking, "There is nothing that I can
do that is big enough to be worth the doing." Let
him remember that spiritual things are not measured

―――――――
* iii. 22-24.

by quantity, but their greatness consists in the purity of their motive. It is one of the greatest glories of this universe that the common and inconspicuous life of ordinary men contains a thousand daily opportunities of spiritual splendor. Says Shri Krishna: "Men reach perfection, each being engaged in his own karma. Better is one's own *dharma*, though inglorious, than the well-performed *dharma* of another. He who does the duty determined by his own state incurs no fault. By worshiping in his own karma (work) him from whom all beings come, him by whom all this is pervaded, a man attains perfection."*

The words of *dharma* and *karma* here require explanation. *Dharma* means where you stand. Each man has to some extent unfolded the flower of his possibility. He stands in a definite position, or holds definite powers of character. It is better that he should recognize his position and be content with it, true to the best he knows, than that he should try to stand in the position of another, or waste his powers in merely envious admiration. To use his powers in the kind of work he *can* do, upon and with the material that his past karma has provided for him in the present, is not only the height of practical wisdom—it is worship of God as well. All life lived in this way is worship; ploughing and reaping, selling and buying—whatever it may be. Conventional forms of kneeling and prostration are not the sole or even the necessary constituents of worship, but every act of the karma yogi and of the *bhakta* is that.

---

* xviii. 45-47 and iii. 35.

The Lord does not ask from his devotees great gifts. Says Krishna: "When anyone offers to me with devotion a leaf, a flower, a fruit or a little water, I accept that, which is brought with devotion by the striving soul. When you do anything, eat anything, sacrifice anything, give anything or make an effort, do it as an offering to me. Thus shall you be released from the bonds of karma, having their good and bad results, and being free and united through *sannyasa* (renunciation) you will come to me. I am alike to all beings; none is disliked by me, and none is favorite; but those who worship me with devotion are in me and I also am in them. Even if a great evil-doer worships me, not devoted to anything else, he must be considered good, for he has determined well. Quickly he becomes a man of *dharma* and attains constant peace. Know, O Son of Kunti, that my devotee never perishes."*

Union With God

As there is community of work between God and man, so is there community of interest, and indeed, community of feeling. "All this is threaded on Me," says the Divine, "like a collection of pearls on a string."† And the reward of the path of yoga is the full realization of this unity: "At the end of many lives the man having wisdom approaches me. 'Vasudeva is all,' says this *Mahatma,* very difficult to find. By devotion he understands me, according to what I

---

* ix. 26-31.
† vii. 7.

really am; then, having truly known me, he enters the boundless. Although always doing work, having me for goal, through my grace he obtains the eternal indestructible goal."*

The love of man for God is more than reciprocated. "He who has no dislike for any being, but is friendly and kind, without greed or egotism, the same in pleasure and pain, forgiving, always content, harmonious, self-controlled and resolute, with thought and affection intent upon me, he, my devotee, is dear to me. He from whom people are not repelled, and who does not avoid the world, free from the agitations of delight, impatience and fear, is dear to me. These devotees who are intent upon the immortal righteousness now declared, full of faith, with me for goal, they are above all dear to me."†

Some of the devotional verses suggest a great absence of self-reliance, *if* they are taken out of their general context, as, for instance: "Giving up all *dharmas* come only to me as your refuge. Do not sorrow; I will release you from all sins." This "I," to whom reference is so often made, is the one Self, the one life, and therefore it advocates the giving up of selfishness and taking interest in the welfare of all. It is a great mistake to think that the *Bhagavad Gita* contains a mixture of teachings, among which one should make a selection. It presents, on the contrary, a coherent philosophy, and a consistent practice for daily life. There is no suggestion anywhere that man should lean upon an external God. His devotion is

---

* vii. 19, and xviii. 55, 56.

† xii. 13-15, 20.

required to the "me" which is *all* life, and not a portion of life in some external form, however grand. Shri Krishna speaks for that one life "equally dwelling in all."* He holds no brief for the worship of limitation, and would not have people go into a cave with a candle to worship the sun. "There is not a being on earth, or among the *devas* in heaven, who is free from the three qualities of Nature."† "Those whose wisdom has been destroyed by personal desires approach other *devas,* having resorted to various observances, following their material natures."‡ "Those who worship the *devas* go to the *devas,* but my devotees come to me."§

Though thus filled with love and work, Krishna's yoga does not neglect the intelligence. It is Krishna who, speaking of the sacrifices that men may make in the service of God for the benefit of man, places at the head of all the use of wisdom. Service is not mere giving. It is giving wisely, and, since wisdom is the treasure that men gather within themselves as the result of many incarnations of work, the offering of wisdom is the greatest of all. Of this Shri Krishna says: "Better than the offering of any material objects is the offering of wisdom, O Parantapa, for all work, O Partha, culminates in wisdom. You should learn this by reverence, inquiry and service, and those who know and see the truth will teach you wisdom. By this you will see all beings without exception in the Self, and thus in me. Even if you were

---

* xiii. 27, 28.
† xviii. 40.
‡ vii. 20.
§ vii. 23, and ix. 25.

the most wicked of evil-doers, you would cross over all sin by the raft of wisdom. As fire reduces fuel to ashes, so does the fire of wisdom reduce all *karmas* to ashes. There is indeed no purifier in the world like wisdom. He who is accomplished finds the same in the Self in course of time. Having attained wisdom he very soon goes to the highest peace."*

The Preliminary Path

This passage introduces us to a portion of the definite path of training—the equivalent of Patanjali's practical yoga. It was not sufficient for Arjuna to have great love. If he would tread the path, he must express it in work in the form of service, and must also have an inquiring mind, so as to gain some understanding. The unbalanced character is unfit for the higher path, no matter how great the progress it may have made along one line. Three practices are prescribed: reverence, inquiry and service—in the original, *pranipata, pariprashna* and *seva.*† The first means bowing, or respect for God in all beings and events, which is the same thing as Patanjali's *ishwara-pranidhana.* The second is inquiry or questioning, something not very different from *swadhyaya.* The third is service, another form of practical effort, the equivalent on this path of Patanjali's *tapas.* The requirements are thus the same in each school, but the order and emphasis varies.

When speaking of service, it is necessary to emphasize broad conceptions. Some would narrow it

---

* iv. 33-39.
† iv. 34.

down to personal service to a particular teacher, but the whole *Gita* points to that brotherhood which is the doing of one's best duty to all around, under any circumstances. The aspirant should desire the welfare of the world. This does not imply that we should merely engage ourselves with those who are in need, who are weak or poor or ignorant, and bestow our assistance upon them. This is a dangerous pastime, as it tends to a habit of superiority, and often ends in the production of a missionary spirit which is fatal to occult progress. Right association with those who are approximately one's equals is, on the whole, the best means for rendering the greatest help to others and oneself. Life does not flow harmoniously across big gaps. The beginner does not become an expert tennis player by playing against great experts, but with those just a little better than himself, and it is not the business of the greatest expert to teach the mere beginner, just as it is not the business of the chief professor of a college to teach the infant class. A good, sensible, brotherly life, in which one does not embarrass others by making conspicuous sacrifices on their behalf, is always the best.

Degrees of Awakening

We may see all mankind in process of evolution or self-unfoldment in seven degrees or stages, according to Shri Krishna's teaching. In the first three stages the man's life is energized from the personality; in the last three, from the higher self; in the middle stage there is a conflict between the two, while the man is beginning to work at the three practices mentioned above.

Modern science recognizes three properties in Nature, or three essential constituents in the objects of the external world. One of these is materiality, or the ability to occupy space, and resist the intrusion of another body into the same space. The second is natural energy, and the third natural law and order. There is no object to be found anywhere, be it large or small, which does not show something of all these three, as it occupies space, shows internal or external energy, and obeys at least some of Nature's laws. These three qualities of Nature were also well known to the ancient Hindus under the names *tamas, rajas,* and *sattwa,* and they held that things differed from one another according to the varied proportions of these three ultimate ingredients. Thus an object in which materiality predominated would be described as *tamasic,* and one in which energy was most prominent would be spoken of as *rajasic.*

The same adjectives are applied very fully in the *Gita* to the personalities of men.* In the early stages of human awakening we have the very material or *tamasic* man, who is sluggish, and scarcely cares to move, unless he is stirred by a strong stimulus from the outside. Next comes the man in whom *rajas* has developed, who is now eager for excitement and full of energy. Perhaps the bulk of people in the world are in this condition. *Rajas* sends them forth into great activity with every kind of greed, from the

---

* xviii.

lowest lust of the body to the highest forms of ambition for wealth and fame and power. Men of this kind cannot restrain themselves—to want is to act.

Thirdly come the people who recognize that there is such a thing as natural law, who realize, for example, that it does not pay to eat and drink just what they like and as much as they like, but that there are certain regulations, about kind and quantity and time, which pertain to eating and drinking, and that violation of these regulations leads to pain. In time that pain draws attention to what is wrong, and the man begins to use his intelligence, first to try to thwart the pain and avert the law, but later on to understand the law, and obey. And then, in that obedience he learns that life is far richer than ever he thought it to be before, that there is in it a sweet strong rhythm unknown to the man of passion, and that alliance with the law can strengthen and enlarge human life beyond all the hopes of the impassioned imagination. All good, thoughtful people are in this third stage, obedient and orderly, and they deserve the name of *sattvic* people.

It is at this point that we find Arjuna in the opening chapter of the *Gita*, when he has sunk down unwilling to fight. Through many experiences and trials, which are described at length in the *Mahabharata*, he has become a man of law and order, but now he rejects the inevitabilities of material life. He says, in effect, "This is not good enough. The natural life is unsatisfying. I must have love, the law of the soul, not of the body." This is the fourth stage, that of struggle.

Shri Krishna tells Arjuna what to do at this moment: "Be thou above the three attributes of Nature, O Arjuna," he says, "beyond the pairs of opposites (such as heat and cold, praise and blame, riches and poverty), ever steadfast in *sattva*, careless of possessions, full of the higher self."* The three qualities of Nature are *tamas, rajas* and *sattva*. The Teacher instructs his pupil to rise above these three, and yet he tells him to establish himself in *sattva*! But *sattva* is obviously one of the three. What then does this mean? There are two kinds of *sattva*, and even of *rajas*, and of *tamas*. *Sattva* is the law and order in things. It is also the law and order in the spiritual life of man; in life there is definite purpose and method, a goal to be attained and a series of experiences which, properly understood, lead to that goal. The man will now learn to understand and obey the spiritual laws.

These laws work out in a multitude of ways in life, but there are three main principles behind them all—principles of the evolution of consciousness. They express themselves in the powers of will, love and thought, creative in the world, and self-creative in the man. There are only three things that the man must now not do. He must never cease to use his will in work. In that work he must never break the law of love. And in that work of love he must never act without using his intelligence. These are principles, greater than all rules and regulations, because they are the living law of the higher self; and not much consideration is required to see that he

_____
* ii. 45.

who follows this law must necessarily show in his practical life all the virtues that are admired by good men of every religion. The man who is established in this *sattva* may be described as in the fifth stage, for the fourth was that period in which the aspirant was raising himself from the *sattva* of Nature to the *sattva* of the higher self by the three practices of reverence, inquiry and service.

The Higher Awakening

Though the man in the fifth stage is unfolding his powers very rapidly, he has not acquired any great momentum. That will come when he reaches the next stage. Then the *rajas*, as it may be called, of the higher self, will come into operation, that fierce, burning love that will brook no obstacle, but *must* express itself in vigorous Karma or Bhakti Yoga. There are men in the third stage who are good men, working steadily for the benefit of their fellows in accordance with the customs and conventions of the form of society in which they find themselves; but the man in the sixth stage is not guided from without. He brings his great energy out from within, and therefore his love has real creative power, and he is able to stand alone in the support of what he thinks to be reforms or in the succor of those who need his help. All the same, this energy from within may often travel into fantastic ways, until the man is more mature in experience of the spiritual life. He is no guide or model for others; only of one thing we can be sure, that in the times when he does not

fall back from the high watermark of his achievement, he at least means well and is unselfish, and
can be counted to sacrifice himself first of all if
he is engaged in a losing cause.

Such a man is capable of considerable agitation
and excitement, because of the rush of energy, not
because outside things can agitate him; but in the
next stage, the seventh, the yogi has reached a state of
serenity. He is now called *yogarudha,* which means
"he who has risen to yoga."* Before that, the aspirant
was only *arurukshu* and *yunjana,* "eager to rise" and
"young at the work." The *tamas* of the higher self
is the spiritual will, that knows itself and can never
be shaken, the quietest and the strongest thing in the
world. He who has reached that place (*yogarudha*—
ascended to yoga) is seated as on a rock, because he
knows in himself that the divine purpose is never
thwarted by anything at all, but is being fulfilled
even in those things that annoy the *yunjana* and the
arurukshu.

These last two stages may also be described in
other terms. The man in the sixth stage, looking at
others, sees looking at him through their eyes a consciousness that is his own. As other men say, "My
house; my money," so this man says, "My other self."
He sees, as Shri Krishna puts it, the same self equally
dwelling in all beings. But the man in the seventh
stage sees more than that—to him all forms are
nothing but very limited expressions of the one life,
toys made for children by children.

---

* iv. 3.

The True Renunciation

There is one term which Shri Krishna applies to all those who are renouncing personal attachment to the objects of the world. He calls them *sannyasis*.* In the last discourse of the *Gita* there is a long explanation of the meaning of the term *sannyasa*. It is compared with another—*tyaga*. *Tyaga* means abandoning, giving up, leaving behind, and the *tyagi* is therefore the man who has renounced the world, given up all possessions, and taken to the uncertain life of a religious mendicant, except perhaps that the term mendicant is not quite appropriate, since this man will not positively beg. *Sannyasa* is the same thing in spirit. As the two *sattwas* are one lower and the other higher, so are *tyaga* and *sannyasa* related to each other. The *sannyasi* does not necessarily give up the material things, but he gives up personal attachment to them.

There is still plenty to do for the man who is becoming more and more conscious of the life around him, and therefore less liable to merely personal motives. The things that he must do are described by Shri Krishna as follows: "Acts of *yajna, dana* and *tapas* should not be given up, but should be done. But even these *karmas* should be done without personal attachment or desire for results."† The three kinds of action which alone the *sannyasi* is permitted to do, and which in fact he must do, are sacrifice, gift and effort.

It is always unsatisfactory to try to translate these

---

* xviii. 5, 6.
† xviii. 49.

technical Sanskrit words into one-word equivalents in English. Sacrifice, (*yajna*) does not mean the mere surrender of things, but it really means to make all things holy. This is done by offering them first to God; or to other men, as the one life is to be recognized as equally dwelling all round. Any action done with an unselfish motive is thus holy. "Eating the remains of sacrifice"* means that the food is offered first to God at the shrine, with suitable words and actions. What he then leaves is considered as from him, and is thus holy. But the *sannyasi* does not perform any ceremony, because he sees the one life everywhere, and all his actions are direct service of that life. In the West it is significant that "holy" is connected with "whole," and so what is done not for selfish gain but in the interests of all is holy. Sacrifice is thus a law by which living beings are related into one great brotherhood.

The *sannyasi* gives freely; leaving it to the law to repay. He also consents to receive only freely, and should anyone offer food or anything else for his use, he declines it if the gift is not sincere, and free from any suggestion of obligation on his part. His life is one of giving (*dana*). All his powers are completely at the service of mankind. And he must strive also, with *tapas*, to increase those powers. There is plenty to do for the man whose life is only sacrifice, gift and effort, whether he be a wandering monk in India or a railroad magnate in the United States.

---

* iii. 13. "Those good people who eat the remains of sacrifice are freed from all guilt, but those who cook for their own sakes eat evil."

Chapter 4

HAPPINESS THROUGH UNDERSTANDING — THE THIRD RAJA YOGA

The Way of Understanding

We now come to the third school of Hindu Raja Yoga, in which the faculty that predominates is thought. The goal of this yoga is realization of the truth about life. The great teacher of this school was Shri Shankaracharya, who, according to Hindu tradition, lived some five hundred years before Christ,* and is regarded by his followers as a special *avatara,* or descent to earth, of the supreme deity Shiva. The prefix Shri is a title of the utmost respect, even of veneration; the suffix *acharya* means a spiritual teacher, and the name Shankara, which is another name of Shiva, means "the producer of happiness."

His yoga is sometimes called the Jnana Yoga, which is what in the West would be called the path of philosophy. The Hindus, however, regard philos-

---

* Western scholars put this about a thousand years later.

ophy as a definite means to human progress and perfection, not simply as an intellectual hobby disconnected from practical life. The pessimism that characterizes the Western world makes people think that there is no ultimate solution to the problems of human poverty, sorrow and strife. The practical Hindu of Krishna's school asserts that the practice of love in feeling and work leads to the solution in the realization of the unity of all life.* Similarly, Western pessimism in science and philosophy suggests that we can never attain the ultimate truth, but the practical Hindus of Shankara's school assert that the way is open, and has been marked out definitely and clearly.

First of all, Shankaracharya makes a distinction between people who want to have and those who want to know. To have is connected with external things. The whole world consists of things to have. Shankara does not deny the infinity of worlds or the existence of "higher planes," containing lofty and glorious beings or gods, or that by desiring things of higher planes or heavens and by worshiping the gods people may obtain centuries and even millenia of delight in various lofty heavens; but he affirms that all those things are the playthings of children or the tinsel of fools, who are making them all for themselves because they have not thought about the eternal realities.

---

* This is as though one were to say to a Christian: "Never mind about interpretations of Christ's words. Do what he said, that is, love your neighbor as yourself. Try it, and that will lead to the greatest good and happiness. That will also take you to him —to his state of being."

He therefore draws a decided distinction between *dharma-jignasa* (the desire to know what should be done in order to obtain better conditions on earth and in heaven) and *Brahma-jignasa* (the desire for that which is eternal) . This is discussed very decisively in Shankara's commentary on the first of the *Brahma-Sutras,* or aphorisms. The desire for the heavens must be preceded by sense-experience, and confidence in the Vedas, which declare that the heavens exist; but the desire for Brahman must be preceded by thought, thought and more thought (*vichara*) , especially with reference to an understanding of the distinction (*viveka*) between the eternal (*nitya*) and temporary (*anitya*) realities. In emphasizing the latter, however, Shankara does not leave out the Vedas, which contain also much advice about seeking the eternal. Shankara's emphasis on thinking is very clear in his *Aparokshanubhuti*: "Thinking should be done for the sake of attaining knowledge of the Self. Knowledge is not attained by any means other than thinking, just as objects are never seen without light. 'Who am I?' 'How is this world produced?' 'Who made it?' and 'What is the material?'—such is the inquiry."*

It is well known that we do not see things as they really are, because of our limited point of view, and yet there is in us the craving for greater understanding, because the human soul is one with the divine or universal soul. Each one of us reflects that, as the disc of the sun may be reflected in many little

---

* *Op. cit.*, 10-12, abridged translation.

pools of water. We have thus a dual nature, and though the lower may be satisfied, still the higher makes its claim in a ceaseless desire to understand. If human power and love were to grow so great as to make our life on earth a perfect paradise of peace and plenty for all, still men would say, "Now, we want to know why all this is so." There are the needs of the personality—food, clothing and shelter, amusement and education, exercise and rest—but beyond these there are spiritual needs, and among them is this real hunger for understanding. It is a spiritual appetite, and its satisfaction results in spiritual growth.

Some ancient peoples thought that the sun traveled every day in a great arc over the earth, because they saw that it did so. Then they reasoned that during the night it must travel back to its starting point in the east through a long tunnel in the bowels of the earth. Now we know that the earth is a ball, and that it is the daily rotation of this ball that is the chief cause of the apparent motion of the sun. It is really the same with every little thing. Thus a tree is a larder to certain kinds of worms; to birds and monkeys it is a house; to the foot passengers on an Indian roadside it is a kind of umbrella; while to a poet or an artist it may suggest a variety of things. It is no easy matter to say, then, what a tree really is. As we usually picture it in imagination, only a side view is seen, and we are apt to forget what it looks like from above, and overlook altogether the part which is beneath the ground. This is true also about ourselves, and the aim of Jnana Yoga is to see man as he truly is. Here is a body, with organs of sense and organs of action, and a conscious being using the body. What is that, and what am I? These are the questions to which our meditation is directed by Shri Shankaracharya.

The Unity of All

The first postulate of this school may be expressed in a saying from one of the Upanishads: *"Sarvam khalwidam Brahma,"* which means "Everything verily is God," or in a sentence from the Rig Veda, *"Ekam sat vipra bahudha vadanti,"* that is, "There is only one Being, though the poets name it variously." Unless all things were at last one united whole, thinking and understanding would be impossible. To realize that one thing, and look at everything in the light of it, is to achieve enlightenment and attain liberation. At one time people thought that the world was made up of a lot of things put together—rocks and water, grass and trees, ants and men; but now it is being realized that all things are parts of one whole, just as a cat is made up of eyes, nose, mouth, claws and tail, and many other parts material and psychical, and yet eyes are only eyes and the tail is only a tail because the cat is a cat. Matter in the form of a tail is not a tail; that would be no tail were it lying by itself on the ground. The part derives from the whole—always.

When a man thinks of himself he makes two big mistakes. First, he thinks of himself imperfectly;

just as the worms think the tree to be merely food, and as the monkeys think it to be a house combined with a gymnasium, he imagines himself to be a male or a female, a doctor or lawyer or merchant or clerk or nurse or housewife, or whatever it may be. Secondly, he forgets that he is not a separate being, but a part of something else, just as the tail is part of the cat. Even external considerations could convince him, if he stopped to examine them, that he is part of the great body of humanity, without the rest of whom he simply would not be what he is in body, feelings or mind, in activity, possessions or knowledge. To put the matter briefly, every time a person puts on any article of clothing he becomes part of a network of beings, comprising millions of people and other creatures. Even earthworms and spiders have played their part in causing him to be what he is, and friends and so-called enemies have both been indispensable. He cannot cut himself off from all that life without becoming zero, physically, emotionally and mentally, but he can rise above his present limitations by understanding the great truth about the unity of all being.

Wisdom

In studying this great truth a man learns wisdom. I may state some points of that wisdom from the *Bhagavad Gita,* for it contains understanding as well as Karma and Bhakti Yogas. No Raja Yoga misses anything of importance, but each has one quality of character as a driving force, or as the leader of the forces of the soul. In the *Gita* you will find it stated that all work culminates in wisdom, and that wisdom is to be obtained by the employment of three means —reverent feelings, an earnest inquiring mind, and acts of service. Shankara's school asserts the same thing. It is not merely knowledge that we are aiming at. Reading, study and meditation will not alone bring realization. There must be *sadhana*—discipline in daily life—as well. There are two great principles at work in the world. One is the active life, building up forms. The other is the great passive principle of Nature, pulling them down. As man works, Nature destroys, yet the fruit of his work is never lost, because it remains in himself as a modification of his character. All the lost work of past civilizations still exists. Though the cities have perished, all the will, love and thought developed in the building of them exists in the character and consciousness of men living today, who are reincarnations of those ancient workers.

Comprehension of this fact should enable a man to reach wisdom with great rapidity. Then, as the *Gita* once more says, the yogi becomes serene. To him, as Emerson put it, "All things are friendly and sacred, all events profitable, all days holy, all men divine." The simple reason for this is that all things serve the soul as means for its experience, clay as well as gold, enemies as well as friends. And he can have no jealousy or envy to whom another's happiness is felt to be as good as his own. That another person should possess something—riches, name, posi-

tion, opportunity, power—is no cause for envy or
desire, for the simple reason that the happiness of
others is the one thing that can give happiness to
those who understand. Such was the kind of life
exemplified by Shankara in his own person, for
though he passed away at the age of thirty-two, he
had done in that short time a life's work for his
fellow-men. He traveled incessantly throughout India, and established four great monasteries to spread
the teaching and practice of Jnana Yoga.

The Meaning of Maya

One of the principal doctrines of this school is
that of *maya,* which has often been translated "illusion," whence it has been thought that the school
teaches that all this world does not exist, and people
only imagine that it does so—that there is nothing
there. That is not so. It does not deny the existence
of objects, but affirms that we see them wrongly,
just as a man may see a piece of rope on the ground
and mistake it for a snake, or as he may see a post
in the distance and think it to be a man. Just as the
Buddha, witnessing the sorrow of mankind, felt that
there must be a solution for it, which he afterwards
discovered; so Shankara, seeing mistakes everywhere,
yet declared that it was possible to realize the truth
behind this *maya.*

It is necessary to know that *maya* has two functions:
"covering-up" (*avritya* or *avarana*) and "throwing-
out" (*vikshepa*) .* The first is declared to be the

---

* See *Shri-Vakhya-Sudha,* 13-19, 35.

effect of *tamas*, which hides or obstructs the life, and the second the result of *rajas,* or material energy.†
"Covering up" implies that although we are every one universal in our essential nature, our attention is now given to less than the whole. Most of the reality is covered up, and since we see only the remainder, it must necessarily become unsatisfying and stupid and even painful, when we have played with it long enough to exhaust its lesson for us. When we have read a book and absorbed the ideas in it, we do not want to read it again. If it is forced upon us, the experience will be painful. I may laugh at a good joke told by a friend today, but if he persists in telling me the same story again and again it will be far from a joke. Our life must be moving and overcoming the *avarana* or *avritti*; there is no pleasure in standing still on any platform of knowledge that we may have gained.

"Covering up" does not mean that objects of experience lack reality. The *maya* or illusion is that we do not see their *full* reality; we see too little, not too much. So far as they go they have an excellent flavor of reality, but their incompleteness is unsatisfying. Suppose, for example, that I am sitting on my verandah when some cows are passing by, and suppose further that by some freak of vision I cannot see the whole of the cows, but only their tails. That procession of tails, perhaps engaged in swinging about and flicking flies, would look very stupid and ridiculous. Yet the tails without the cows are real enough. As the *Gita* puts it: "The unreal has no being."

---

† See *Viveka-Chudamani,* 113, 115.

The second function of *maya,* "throwing-out" (*vik-shepa*), means that we put forth our creative energy in reference to that part of reality which for us individually has not been covered up, and thereby we produce the world of *maya* or created things, which are only temporary (*anitya*). The origin of the word *maya* is difficult to explain, but its significance appears very clearly in certain compound words, in which it has the meaning of making or creation. Thus, for example, we say *mano-maya-kosha,* or body made of thought, that is, mind. We can also speak in Sanskrit of a bag made of leather, using the same term *maya* in the compound word. This being the case, one cannot say that *maya* indicates pure illusion, in the sense that the object has no reality, but it means that the idea that tails can go about with no cows attached to them is an illusion. In other words, to see the world as a material world is false.

The power of "throwing-out" is not merely of the mind, but it is actually creative, and this it is which makes all the forms around us, the world of manifestation. The objects therein are very much like pictures painted by an artist. They represent his expression of such part of the reality as is not covered up. As he looks at the picture and realizes how defective and even nonsensical it is, the hunger arises in him for something more satisfying, which then works at removing the "covering-up." Thereby arises what is called intuition, which always comes as the result of a complete study of any fact or group of facts in the world of experience. It is in this manner that experience is educative. It gives us nothing from the outside, but enables us to introduce ourselves to a fuller part of reality.

Realization of Reality

The question then arises—what is the best way to attain reality? To this I think two answers may be given: (1) Realize the infinite possibilities of every finite experience, and (2) do not mix yourself with your objects of experience. As to the first, it means simply that we can learn from one thing what we can learn from many things. The following appears to me to be a clear example. If in the course of my life I have learnt to love my mother, then I am capable of loving any mother whom I may meet. I do not need to learn the lesson all over again in connection with those other mothers. As instructed in the *Gita*, by attending to my own experience I can reach perfection. But I must remember that that occurs only if I respect and even reverence experience—all of it, every bit of it that happens to come my way. The uncovering which results from this can very soon show us further possibilities.

Another instance of the same principle is the use of the human body. If we had to attain some kind of perfection which involved knowledge of everything that is going on, or experience of all things which people are making for themselves by their "throwing-out," this body would not be enough. In such a case we should need a hundred or a thousand arms and legs instead of only two of each. But this is not the way of the evolution of life. It can reach its perfection through an ordinary body with two arms and two legs. It need not have the muscular system of a professional athlete or the mental capacity of a German chemist or lexicographer. Realize the infinite possibilities of the moment's experience, cease to resent any of the experience, and immediately most of the pain and sorrow that it may contain is emptied out of it, and it becomes immensely fruitful.

There are two ways in which we may live our lives amidst events of the world, without retiring at all from that world. In both cases the mixing with the world will be the same, but in one there is real confusion (that is fusing together) and in the other merely mixing. For example, if milk and water are put together it is very difficult to separate them, but if oil and water are mixed together, although they are together they retain their individuality. So in relation to the world we should be like oil in water, not milk in water. We must distinguish between "the world," "my world" and "myself"—three things, not two. It is like a person playing a game of chess. The board is there—my world. The pieces have been moved into a certain position. A good player does not become excited and flustered, whether he is winning or losing. He cannot, in fact, really in himself either win or lose. Even if his pieces are taken one by one, if he has played the game to the best of his ability he has developed his faculties, and on the whole he is a little more likely to profit by a lost than by a won game.

These facts being established, people sometimes raise the academic question: "Whence comes this ignorance which hides the full reality?" With regard to this it may be remembered that Buddha's advice was: "Sink not the string of thought into the fathomless." The fact is we have to begin our reasoning and our activity from the place in which we find ourselves. We are apparently on a ladder, which goes upward out of sight. The important thing is that it goes upward. But one would not avoid the ultimate question. I believe that the answer to it is that space and time are a creation of ignorance, they come into being through the "covering-up," and disappear for us when the covering is removed. How, then, can the questions "where" and "whence," which ask for an answer in terms of time and space, be applied to this matter? Evidently there is evolution or unfoldment, but it is not a change in time and space. That this is so is indicated by the unchanging character of our feeling of "I," which is the same point of reference in youth and age, and whether we be here or there, and standing on our heads or on our feet.

Shankaracharya speaks in very strong language about the effect of *avriti* and *vikshepa* in practical life: "The function of *avriti,* made of *tamas,* covers up the shining Self, which has unlimited faculties; just as the shadow of the moon hides the disc of the sun. When there is thus the obscuration of a man's real and stainlessly radiant Self, he thinks he is the body, which is not the Self. Then the great power of *rajas* called *vikshepa* afflicts him by the binding qualities of passion, anger, etc.; so that this unintelligent man, deprived of real knowledge of the Self, through being swallowed by the crocodile of the great delusion, wanders about, rising and falling in the ocean of limited existence. As clouds produced by the sun obscure the sun as they develop, so does egotism arising from the Self obscure the Self as it flourishes. And as on a bad day when thick clouds swallow the sun, and they also are afflicted by sharp cold winds, so does the power of acute *vikshepa* annoy the man of confused intelligence with many troubles. By these two powers the man is bound; deluded by them he wanders about, thinking the body to be himself."*

Then comes the question how to remove these two: "Unless the *avarana* function ceases completely, *vikshepa* cannot be conquered. When subject and object are separated, like milk from water, then *avarana* disappears on its own account in the Self. Perfect discrimination, arising from clear perception, having distinguished the subject and the object, cuts away the bondage of delusion made by *maya,* and then for the free man there is no more wandering about."†

The substance of material things is called *sat,* or being. Consciousness, with its powers of will, love and thought, is called *chit.* Then beyond those three aspects of consciousness is *ananda,* the true life that is sheer happiness. The being of true life is happiness. First a man must get over the delusion that he is the body, and realize that he is consciousness using the body. He *has* a body. Then, later on, he must

---

* *Viveka-Chudamani,* 141-146, abridged translation.

† *Ibid.,* 345-348, abridged translation.

realize that he is not the powers of consciousness, but that he simply uses these. Then he will be his own true self, *ananda,* happiness, which is the nature of our pure being. But that *ananda* is one with *chit* and *sat,* as the man will find on reaching illumination; so the world of *sat* is real, part of his own true life, and not illusion. *Maya* was the practical effect of the mistake (*avidya*) by which he confused together, first consciousness and external being, and later consciousness and his own being.

The analogy of dreaming is employed to illustrate these points. Just as on waking we realize that our dream was irrational, so on waking from the dream that we now call waking we shall realize the truth that will make our present outlook appear irrational. Not that it is irrational, but that the true vision is far more rational. Even our present knowledge, it is said, is ignorance, or better unwisdom, because we are always looking at things with the eyes of the flesh, while we ought to look at them with the eyes of the spirit, that is, from the standpoint of the imperishable consciousness.

Meditation on the Self

The meditations of Shankara are practical, because they are not merely thoughts about things, considered as objects, dwelt upon in the third grammatical person. First, the student must say to himself, "I am not *it*"—"it" being the personality, physical and psychical, composed of body, personal emotions and fixed ideas, not simply the set of "vehicles" as they stand, but also their habits of action, emotion and thought—the entire personality. He must put that outside himself. Secondly, he must say, "I am not *you*," referring now to that in himself which he would call you in another person—the collection of powers of consciousness. The personality is something that you use—not something that you are. So also the conscious powers are something that you use, not something that you are. Thirdly, he must say, "I am I. I can take up and put down consciousness. I can enlarge or reduce consciousness." But in the second stage he must take care to think of his own consciousness always as *you*, never as *it*, otherwise he will remain in the *you*, and not reach the *I*.

All happiness in life is beyond consciousness and is experienced when consciousness is forgotten. All the delight that comes from response to beauty, love and truth in the world, and from the powers of will, love and thought in consciousness, lie in the Self beyond, when the world and consciousness are forgotten, and time and space have been swallowed up in something greater, beyond their limitations. Beyond consciousness, in a state better than consciousness, I am, and all clinging to consciousness, like clinging to body, bars the realization of that truth. That *I* is *ananda*, happiness, the one reality. To the Buddhist it is *nirvana*. The *atma* or Self denied by Buddha as an ultimate reality, stated by him to be not that which is ·eternal, was but the will, an aspect of consciousness. It was not the same thing as the *atma* or Self, of Shankaracharya.

The Preliminary Steps

For the realization of this, or even the desire to realize it, what is called *sadhana,* or practice, is supremely important. In this school, as in the others, the work is divided into a preliminary and an advanced course, and once more the preliminary course is a kind of general education, requiring a certain training and direction of thought, love and will—all three. It is interesting to make a comparison of the three schools in this respect. It will be seen from the following table that the same three things are taught in each, but that to Patanjali the will is the chief means, while to Krishna it is love, and to Shankara it is thought.

PATANJALI	KRISHNA	SHANKARA
1. *Tapas* (Will)	1. *Pranipata* (Love)	1. *Viveka* (Thought)
2. *Swadhyaya* (Thought)	2. *Pariprashna* (Thought)	2. *Vairagya* (Love)
3. *Ishwara- pranidhana* (Love)	3. *Seva* (Will)	3. *Shatsampatti* (Will)

The Use of Thought

The three means in this general training lead to the awakening in the personality of a complete response to the three powers of consciousness—thought, love and will. The requirement first mentioned is *viveka,* discrimination, discernment, insight.* It comes from the practice of meditation upon the personality, so that life in it may henceforth be the positive life of the indwelling consciousness, and not simply a succession of conscious states called into expression by personal stimuli. This meditation is threefold. First, one must dwell upon the body and realize that it is only an instrument for the conscious self to play upon. Then, one must dwell on the habits of feeling and emotion which have been accumulated during the present lifetime (or strictly, body-time) and realize these also to be part of the instrument—"I am surely not my feelings and emotions toward things and people." Thirdly, one must meditate upon the fact that the lower mind, the collection of information, ideas and opinions that one has acquired up to this period, is also not the self, but merely an internal library more or less imperfectly indexed, in which the books have a tendency to open at certain places because they have been opened there many times before.

This meditation must then be applied to other people, so that one comes to think of them as the consciousness beyond the personality, and in dealing with them to assist and further the higher purposes of the Self within them rather than the desires rising from the personality. Being a material thing, even up to the mental plane, that personality has its own quality of inertia, and dislikes the discomfort involved in new thinking and willing and feeling, until

* *Viveka-Chudamani,* 18-28.

it is well trained and learns to rejoice in the sharing of a life more than its own. But we must help to bring the day of triumph nearer for all whom we contact, as Shri Shankara did.

The meditation must be extended still further to all the business of life, to the family, the shop, the field, the office, society. All these things must be considered as of importance not as they minister to the laziness, selfishness or thoughtlessness of the personality, but as they bear on the advancement in power of will, love and thought of the evolving consciousness in all concerned.

Fifteen to thirty minutes of this kind of meditation each day is sufficient to establish an entirely new outlook in the personality. Emerson speaks of something of the same kind in his essay on "Inspiration," as the way to an altogether richer life than any of us can possibly reach without it. It can often be practiced to some extent under unfavorable conditions, as for example in the railway train, if one makes up one's mind to take the various disturbances of it with a sweet temper, and lend oneself to the rhythm of its noise.

The Use of Emotions

The second requirement is *vairagya,* an emotional condition in which one does not respond at once to impressions coming from the outer world, but first submits the matter to the discriminative power rising from *viveka.* If you strike an ordinary man, he will get hot and strike back, or run away, or do something else spontaneous and scarcely rational; but a man having *vairagya* would use his spiritual intelligence before responding. The literal meaning of the word *vairagya* is "absence of color," and in this connection it means absence of passion. *Raga* is coloring, especially redness. People everywhere take their emotional coloring from their environment, according to well known psychological laws; like pieces of glass placed on blue or red or green paper, they change their color. Likes and dislikes rise up in them without reason, at the mere sight of various objects, and the appearance of different persons calls up pride, anger, fear, and the other personal emotions.

They are constantly judging things not with their intelligence, but by their feeling and emotional habits. "This is good, that is bad," means generally nothing more than, "I like this; I do not like that." A man dislikes a thing because it disturbs his physical or emotional convenience or his comfortable convictions, "I thought I had done with thinking about that—take it away, confound you," grumbles the man comfortably settled in his opinions, as in a big armchair. There was once a workman who loved his home after a fashion, and used to spend his evenings there. "Give me my armchair before the fire of an evening," he used to say, "a newspaper and a pot of beer and my pipe, and I would not call the Queen my aunt!" The *vairagi* sees no intrinsic value in beer and tobacco and newspaper, or any other thing, but cherishes the living power of love, will and thought that he feels pulsating within himself, and sees flashing into life now and then in the people around him.

Vairagya is the absence of agitation due to things outside. A mistaken idea which is sometimes associated with this word is that it implies absence of emotion. That is not so. The purified personality responds to the higher emotions, the love emotions that belong to the real self. Those emotions come from that aspect of the indwelling consciousness which feels the other life to be as interesting as one's own. This is the root of all the love emotions—admiration, kindness, friendship, devotion and others—which must not be confused with any sort of passion, which is personal or bodily desire. If a man has *vairagya* and he is still emotional, his emotion must be some form of love.

Vairagya may be developed by a form of meditation in which the aspirant should picture and turn over in his mind the various things that have been causing him agitation, or the disturbing emotions of pride, anger and fear. Having made a picture of the cat spilling the ink on the best tablecloth, or of your enemy putting in a bad word for you with your employer or superior behind your back, you calmly in the midst of it all change the emotion that rises, and picture yourself as acting without agitation.

This is a question of feeling, not of action. Do not here substitute the deadly coldness that some people sometimes feel instead of anger, and imagine that to be the calm state; but meditate upon the scene and decide what the right emotion would be if you understood what the whole matter meant to the Self, and if you also understood what effect your own action would have in turn upon the spiritual progress of the man whom you want to kick.

The calmness obtained in this way will soon make all the other meditation far more effective than before, because meditation best opens the door to the inner world and all its inspiration when the body is quiet, the emotions are calm, and the attention is turned without any muscular or nervous strain or physical sensation whatever to the subject of thought. Incidentally it should be said that meditation with physical sensation or strain may prove injurious to health, but meditation rightly done in this way can never do the least harm.

The Use of Will

The third requirement is called *shatsampatti,* which may be translated "the six forms of success." The will is now used to make all conditions favorable for the further development of *viveka.* To understand the function of the will, it is necessary to realize that it is the faculty with which we change ourselves. Thought is *kriyashakti,* the power that acts upon matter; but it is will with which we change our thoughts and other inward conditions. Now will power is used to bring the whole life of the man within the purpose of Jnana Yoga. This work is the equivalent of the *tapas* of Patanjali and the *seva* of Krishna.

The six forms of success are: (1) *shama,* control of mind, resulting in calmness; (2) *dama,* control of body; (3) *uparati,* which means cessation from eagerness to have certain persons and things around one, and therefore a willing acceptance of what the world offers, contentment with regard to things and tolerance with regard to persons, a glad acceptance of the material available for life's work. The fourth is *titiksha,* patience, the cheerful endurance of trying conditions and the sequence of karma. The fifth is *shraddha,* fidelity and sincerity, and therefore confidence in oneself and others. The sixth is *samadhana,* steadiness, with all the forces gathered together and turned to the definite purpose in hand.

Every one of these qualities shows the will at work producing that calm strength which is its own special characteristic. This is necessary for yoga, and anything in the nature of fuss, or push, or excitement is against it. In no case does this calmness mean the reduction of activity or work, but always that the work is done with greater strength but less noise. Success is marked by quietness, the best indication of power. Thus the mind and body will be active but calm; and there will be contentment, patience, sincerity and steadiness.

The three branches of training already mentioned make the entire personality exceedingly sensitive to the higher self, so that a great longing arises for a fuller measure of realization. This is called *mumukshatwa,* eagerness for liberty.

CHAPTER 5

THE FOUR HATHA YOGAS

The aims of Hatha Yoga vary, insomuch as for some it is to spend long years in a happy heaven or in the company of the desired form of God, but for others it is the same as that of the Raja Yogis, who wish to be fully conscious of the one life in which all forms of existence have their being, like clouds in the sky. But all Hatha Yoga works agree in declaring that external practices are necessary for the quickest possible attainment of the goal. There is sometimes a discussion as to whether external means are essential or not, but *if* it were true that they are useful for the development of the man himself (which I think is not the case) they would obviously be essential to those who wished to produce in themselves the most rapid awakening. One of the standard works, the *Shiva Samhita* argues: "There is no Hatha Yoga without Raja Yoga and no Raja Yoga without Hatha; therefore the Yogi should start with Hatha Yoga, guided by a competent teacher."*

---

* *Op. cit.,* v. 181.

I must not refer to any of these Hatha Yoga practices without sounding a severe warning. Many people have brought upon themselves incurable illness and even madness by practicing them without providing the proper conditions of body and mind. The yoga books are full of such warnings, and they tell the would-be practitioner to go to a teacher who really knows all about these things, to receive personal inspection and instruction. For example, the *Gheranda Samhita* announces that if one begins the practices in hot, cold or rainy weather, diseases will be contracted, and also if there is not moderation in diet, for only one half the stomach must ever be filled with solid food.* When I tried the long breathing, as a boy of fourteen or fifteen, for three quarters of an hour, I found when I stood up that I had lost my sense of touch and weight. I handled things without feeling them, and walked without any sense of touching the ground. The sense returned after ten or fifteen minutes, but I dropped the practice.

Let us turn to the Hatha Yoga proper, whose method employs chiefly the regulation of breathing.

The *Hatha Yoga Pradipika* states that control of breath must be brought about very gradually, "as lions, elephants and tigers are tamed," or "the experimenter will be killed," and by any mistake there arises cough, asthma, head, eye and ear pains, and many other diseases.† On the other hand, right practice may be undertaken by anybody, even the young

---

* *Op. cit.*, v. 8, 16, 22.

† *Op. cit.*, ii. 15-18, and i. 15. The *Sandilya Upanishad* gives the same warning.

and the old, the sick and the weak, and will result in slenderness and brightness of body.†

The theory behind these breathing exercises is that between the mind and the body comes *prana*. This word is translated "breath," but various descriptions of its five kinds operating in various parts of the body would indicate that it means not only the ordinary breathing, but also some other functions of air in the body, or perhaps of etheric currents of some kind. However, in practice, the first two, the principal forms of breath are associated with the inbreathing and outbreathing. Therefore it is considered that the regulation of breath will govern the body, which will then react upon the mind.

Some teachers maintain that all the impurities of the body may be removed merely by control of breath, but others hold that it is necessary to practice certain cleansings, especially in the case of persons who are flabby and phlegmatic.*

I should like to make it clear that I am not recommending these practices, as I hold that all Hatha Yogas are extremely dangerous, and they are unnecessary, because Raja Yoga will bring about a correct mental and emotional condition, and purity and health of the body will gradually follow upon that. The science of health is always more important than the science of curing disease, and external curing lacks permanent effect, unless the causes of troubles are also attended to. The Raja Yoga is undoubtedly correct in laying down first morality based on respect

---

† *Ibid.*, i. 64 and ii. 20.
* *Hatha Yoga Pradipika*, ii. 37, 21.

for life in others, and then the guidance and use of mind. Especially must the reader be warned against sensationalists and money-makers in these matters, and against those who sell "secrets" of yoga which may be a hash made from translations of Hindu yoga literature.

Closely connected with the elaborate practices of *pranayama* are the postures. Quite often eighty-four of these are enumerated, but the *Shiva Samhita* contents itself with recommending four, which are called "The Adept Seat," "The Lotus Seat," "The Powerful Seat," and "The Swastika Seat." These are briefly as follows: (1) body straight, legs crossed, one heel at the anus, the other at the front, gaze between the eyebrows, chin on breast;* (2) legs folded with feet, soles upward, on opposite thighs, arms crossed, hands on thighs, tongue pressed against teeth, chin on breast or held up, gaze on tip of nose; or arms may be crossed behind, hands holding great toes;† (3) legs stretched out, apart, head held in hands and placed on knees;‡ (4) feet between calves and thighs, body straight.§ The *Hathayoga Pradipika* also advocates four *asanas* especially, two being the same and two different.

The Laya Yoga

The two great features of the Laya Yoga are *Kundalini* and the *chakras*. *Kundalini* is described as a

* *Shiva Samhita*, iii. 85; *Gheranda S.* ii. 7, 8; *Hathayoga P.* i. 36.
† *Shiva Samhita*, iii. 88; *Gheranda S.* ii. 9; *Hathayoga P.* i. 45, 46.
‡ *Shiva Samhita*, iii. 92; *Gheranda S.* ii. 23; *Hathayoga P.* i. 29.
§ *Shiva Samhita*, iii. 95; *Gheranda S.* ii. 14; *Hathayoga P.* i. 20.

force lying in three and a half coils, like a sleeping serpent, in a cavity near the base of the spine. This is regarded as a goddess, "luminous as lightning," who, even though sleeping, maintains all living creatures. She lies there with her head blocking a fine channel which goes straight up the spine and is known as the *sushumna*.

The purpose of the Laya Yoga practice is to awaken the *Kundalini* (or "coiled one"), who will start up hissing, and can then be carried through the series of six *chakras* (literally, "wheels"), which are threaded upon that channel at various points in the body, which are situated at the level of the base of the spine, the root of the penis, the navel, the heart, the throat and the eyebrows. These *chakras* are depicted somewhat as flowers rather than wheels, and have petals respectively numbering four, six, eight, twelve, sixteen, and two.

Each *chakra* has its own diagram, colors, animals, divinities, letters, etc. It will be evident that the yogi, as he meditates in each of them in the course of his progress, will have plenty to think about. Arthur Avalon's excellent translation of the *Shatchakra Nirupana*, with comments thereon,* is a mine of information on the subject, but the thorough student should also read various minor Upanishats, Puranas and general works on yoga touching on this subject. There is a certain amount of conflicting testimony on the subject of colors, divinities, etc., but this does not mar the general unity of information as regards

---

* *The Serpent Power*, by Arthur Avalon. Published by Ganesh & Co., Madras.

all the main features.†

The way in which the yogi wraps himself up in a world of his own imagining, when meditating in these *chakras,* is shown in the following verses, which I translated from the Gheranda Samhita for my book on *Concentration:*

> Let him find in his heart a broad ocean of nectar,
>   Within it a beautiful island of gems,
> Where the sands are bright golden and sprinkled
>   with jewels,
>   Fair trees line its shores with a myriad of blooms,
> And within it rare bushes, trees, creepers and rushes,
>   On all sides shed fragrance most sweet to the sense.
>
> Who would taste of the sweetness of divine
>   completeness
>   Should picture therein a most wonderful tree,
> On whose far-spreading branches grow fruit of all
>   fancies—
>   The four mighty teachings that hold up the world.
> There the fruit and the flowers know no death and
>   no sorrows,
>   While to them the bees hum and soft cuckoos sing.
>
> Now, under the shadow of that peaceful arbor
>   A temple of rubies most radiant is seen.
> And he who shall seek there will find on a seat rare,
>   His dearly Beloved enshrined therein.
> Let him dwell with his mind, as his teacher defines,
>   On that Divine Form, with his modes and his signs.

---

† The *Yoga Kundali Upanishat* gives sixteen petals in the heart center, instead of twelve, and the *Dhyanabindu Upanishat* and the *Shandilya Upanishat* both describe the navel *padma* as having twelve petals instead of ten.

This particular meditation takes place in a small subsidiary *chakra* just below the twelve-petaled lotus of the heart, so it does not contain such a variety of symbology as is usually brought in.

There is a poetical rather than an exact description of what happens as Kundalini rises. The spine is called "the axis of creation" for the body. In that is the channel *sushumna;* within that another, named *vajroli,* and within that again another, called *chitrini,* "as fine as a spider's thread." On this tube the lotuses are said to be threaded "like knots on a bamboo rod." Kundalini rises up little by little, as the yogi employs his will. In one practice he brings her as far as he can, and, as she pierces any one of the lotuses, its face, which was turned downwards before, turns upwards, and when the meditation is finished he leads her back to her home near the base of the spine.* It is held that as she leaves each *chakra* on the way up, she withdraws the functions of that center, and so makes them latent (hence the term Laya Yoga, or the Yoga of Suspension). It is, of course, natural that in such a process, as attention is given more and more to the higher thought, the lower responses should become latent, as, for example, when we are reading and do not hear or see a person who enters the room.

---

* There is a little difference of opinion here. Some hold that once she has reached the heart *chakra,* that will be her permanent home, and she will not return below it. Others say that even from the beginning she was at the level of the navel. These are not altogether reasonable views, if, as is usually believed, Kundalini has the work of purifying and transmuting all the lower centers on her return journey from the higher.

Kundalini proceeds upwards until she reaches the great "thousand-petaled lotus" at the top of the head, beyond all the six *chakras*. There she enjoys the bliss and power of union with the source of all life, and afterwards, as she returns through the *padmas,* she gives back to each its specific powers, purified and enhanced. The process of bringing Kundalini to the highest point is usually considered to require some years, but there are exceptional cases in which it is done quickly.

The Hatha Yoga books take up a curious view of the mind in relation to all these matters. It is expressed in a few verses of the *Hathayoga Pradipika.* "The mind is the lord of the senses; the breath is the lord of the mind; and that depends on *nada.*"* "There is talk of *laya, laya,* but what is its character? Laya is the non-arising of further *vasanas,*‡ and the forgetting of external things."† Some of the minor Upanishats, such as the "Muktika" of the "Shukla-Yajurveda", have a similar idea.

Samadhi, the highest practice of yoga, is conceived in a very material manner in the Hatha Yoga books. The idea is that the yogi in *samadhi* is uninfluenced by anything external, because the senses have become inactive, and he does not even know himself or others.§ Although the *Gheranda Samhita* says that *samadhi* involves union of the individual with the

---

* *Hathayoga Pradipika,* iv. 29.

‡ The "perfume" of past attachments or desires, which now produces pleasure and pain; if I may use a crude simile, like the smell of onions long after they have been eaten.

† *Ibid.,* iv. 34.

§ *Op. cit.,* iv. 109.

supreme Self (*Paratman*), so that "I am Brahma and no other; Brahma am I, without any sorrows; I am of the nature of fundamental existence, knowledge and bliss, always free and self-supporting,"† it also prescribes for attainment of this various *mudras* or physical practices, such as that of turning the tongue into the nasal cavity and stopping the breath,‡ the theory being that all you need to do is to cut off contact with this world, and the other state will be there.

This view places the value of physical life and experience at zero. But pure Raja Yoga implies realization of one's divine being and power in the midst of external events, the retirements of meditation being intended for the gathering of strength of love, thought or will. It is not denied that breath and mind, and body and mind influence each other intimately; so much is it the case that what is reached at any time in intuition must have its creative or modifying effect in the organs of consciousness in the body. The *Gita* points out that ordinary men, thinking about sense-objects, become attached to them; from this arises desire for them, and that, frustrated, produces anger; anger produces excitement and this destroys memory;* then comes loss of *buddhi* (perception of life, or feeling for others) and thus he perishes. But the self-controlled man goes about among the objects of sense without being attracted or repelled by them, and so he attains peace.§

---

† *Op. cit.*, vii. 3, 4.
‡ *Ibid.*, vii. 7 *et seq.*
* The man "loses his head."
§ *Op. cit.*, ii. 64, 65.

The Yoga of Devotion

In the list which I have made of seven forms of yoga, it will have been noticed that there is a certain correspondence between numbers 3 (Jnana) and 5, (Laya) insomuch as they proceed mainly through intelligence and understanding rather than through feeling or determination. The difference between them lies chiefly in the application of the intelligence, which in number 3 is directed mostly to the internal consciousness, and in number 5 to the various centers in the body, as the subtle organs of abnormal vision and powers, and as the gateways which, some hold, can best and most quickly be opened from the outside, to higher states of consciousness.

When we come to consider feeling, we find the same relation between the Karma Yoga (number 2) and the Bhakti Yoga (number 6). Both represent forms of love; the former rises out of love of human and other companionate lives, and the latter from love of God. Some readers having just a little knowledge of the yogas may find my placing of the love of men as internal and the love of God as external somewhat surprising at first sight, but this is the only sound classification. Karma Yoga means union by work or service, but behind that is what Shri Krishna, in the *Bhagavad-Gita*, calls Buddhi Yoga, which I would translate, "the Yoga of perceiving the life."*

---

* *Op. cit.*, ii. 49-53. Buddhi Yoga is taught, and then, in verse 50, the teacher says, "Yoga is skill in karmas," while in verses 51-53 he explains that in all this work or activity there will be no desire for the material results of work, because the man never loses his perception of the life.

Karma Yoga is only an expression of Buddhi Yoga, which means that the yogi is able to feel the life or consciousness of others, which is always much more interesting than mere material objects, which are, so to speak, the thrown-off creations of the life, employed for external purposes and the mere satisfaction of the body.

To know the life in others is to love it, just as we all find fascinating the unfolding psychology in little animals and children, whose pretty ways are delightful because we see the life expressing itself. In those cases perception of the life is not shrouded for us by any sense of personal danger, and the fear and dislike are aroused in us in the presence of power which may be detrimental to our physical well-being or at least to our comfort. A snake is very interesting and beautiful, but many people shudder with horror at the sight of it. We should also view our pet animals differently if they were several sizes larger.

This love of the life in all, which leads to service of mankind, is internal because it acknowledges no barriers; its primal unconscious interest is in the increase of our being through adding to it the life all around, in contrast with that of the unawakened man, who is interested in the enhancement of his personal sensations or in the enlargement of his personality through increase of possessions or the enjoyment of power. In the *Bhagavad Gita* there is much talk of devotion (*bhakti*) to God as well as to man, but this is quite different from common *bhakti,* for it demands the recognition of the one life, and com-

plete devotion to that which is seated in the hearts
of all. This I have shown very clearly in chapter 3.
Common *bhakti,* which the *Gita* does not advocate,
thinks of God as a particular being, not the life in
all, and of "him" or "her" (as the case may be) as
reachable through an external form, or as giving
some benefits which the man is unable to obtain
or to reach through the use of his own best powers
of consciousness.

The Hindus have collective, though not organized,
worship, in the form of *bhajanas,* in which songs are
sung, containing mostly the names of the deities, to
the accompaniment of drums and music, before a
statue or a picture representing the divinity. Individual worship appears in daily prayers and in yoga
practice.

Why is a separate or outside God adored, reverenced, worshipped? Because he is regarded as the
source of wealth and bounty, considered either as an
example, or as a giver of material benefits, or at
least of divine "grace." Such leaning on externals is
contrary to all Raja Yoga. The goal of our being is
upright, strong life, happy and free because it is
illuminated as to its own divine nature and that of
all the other lives seen around, using other forms.
If, then, the goal of life is this happiness, which is
the joy of upright, strong life, master of its own
small world of body and circumstances, how can it
be said that anybody is helped toward that freedom
at any stage by the intoxications or consolations of
religion, when it is conceived of as offering a refuge

or a protection given by some other being? Let a man do his small daily task according to his strength of will, love and thought, and all will be well with him. He can be immensely devoted to all the life around him, regarding his neighbor as himself. His refuge from selfishness and the fear it brings exists, but he should not bring into it the unnatural considerations of another, and separate life governing and uplifting his own.

As I have already remarked, the various Hatha Yogas are very much mixed together. Devotion, therefore, comes in, along with concentration in the various *chakras,* and the *Gheranda Samhita* mentions it as one of the means to *samadhi*: "Let him meditate in his own heart upon the proper form of his desired deity; let him meditate with the Bhakti Yoga, full of the greatest gladness; let him shed tears of happiness."*

The flow of unrestrained feeling, even if it means self-abandonment before the recognized glory of the divine, also has its dangers, as the insane asylums testify all over the Western world, and a red record of war and cruelty witnesses in history, although it is a path that may be followed without special guidance, provided the development of intelligence and will in practical life is not seriously neglected. Many churches and other organizations are busy on this line, but for the most part they miss the point of it because they direct attention to God or his representative as something for the weakling to lean upon

---

* *Op. cit.,* vii. 14-15.

or as a fountain of blessings for personal gratification, rather than as something so splendid that at the mere sight of it one loses personal desires completely, forgets oneself in the contemplation of it, and adds a new form of ecstasy to the permanent treasures of the soul.

The Mantra Yoga

The Mantra Yoga is that in which the chief feature is the repetition (*japa*) of certain fixed forms of words, often with a definite intonation, and always with the thought of their meaning and intention. We find this frequently combined with the Bhakti Yoga, as in the following example, which I translated some years ago, with explanations, from the *Gopalatapani Upanishad* and the *Krishna Upanishad*. Of all the mantras of Shri Krishna, none is considered more powerful than this five-divisioned, eighteen-syllabled one, which is: *"Klim Krishnaya, Govindaya, Gopi-jana, Vallabhaya Swaha!"*

"Once the sages came to the great Brahma and asked: 'Who is the supreme God? Whom does Death fear? Through the knowledge of what does all become known? What makes this world continue on its course?'

"He replied: 'Shri Krishna verily is the supreme God. Death is afraid of Govinda (Shri Krishna). By knowledge of the Lord of Gopi-jana (Shri Krishna) the whole is known. By Swaha the world goes on evolving.'

"Then they questioned him again: 'Who is Krishna? Who is Govinda? Who is the Lord of Gopi-jana? What is Swaha?'

"He replied: 'Krishna is he who destroys all wrong. Govinda is the knower of all things, who, on earth, is known through the great teaching. The Lord of Gopi-jana is he who guides all conditioned beings. Swaha is his power. He who meditates on these, repeats the mantra, and worships him, becomes immortal.'

"Again they asked him: 'What is his form? What is his mantra? What is his worship?'

"He replied: 'He who has the form of a protector of cows. The cloud-colored youth. He who sits at the root of the tree. He whose eyes are like the full-blown lotus. He whose raiment is of the splendor of lightning. He who is two-armed. He who is possessed of the sign of wisdom. He who wears a garland of flowers. He who is seated on the center of the golden lotus. Who meditates upon him becomes free. His is the mantra of five parts. The first is *Klim Krishnaya. Klim* is the seed of attraction. The second is *Govindaya*. The third is *Gopijana*. The fourth is *Vallabhaya*. The fifth and last is *Swaha*. *Klim*—to Krishna—to the Giver of Knowledge—to the Lord of the Cowherds—*Swaha*!'"

"Om. Adoration to the Universal Form, the Source of all Protection, the Goal of Life, the Ruler of the Universe, and the Universe itself.

"Om. Adoration to the Embodiment of Wisdom, the Supreme Delight, Krishna, the Lord of Cowherds! To the Giver of Knowledge, adoration!"

Such mantras as this are full of symbology. The word *krishna* means the color of the rain-cloud, a symbol of protection and beneficence. The cows are the verses of scripture. *Vallabha* means Lord and also Beloved, and the "cowherd people" are the great sages. The tree is creation or evolution.

The recitation of the Vedas, when it is performed by a great many pandits at once, has a most moving effect upon almost any audience. In many ways the rituals of the Catholic churches among the Christians closely resemble in their methods of worship the Hindu practices of both Bhakti and Mantra Yogas.

There is also what is called the *Ajapa Gayatri,* which is described in many places. It simply means that one should think that with every breath one is saying *So'ham,* meaning "I am That." The breath comes in with the sound "sa" and goes out with the sound "ha," and of these movements there are said to be twenty-one thousand six hundred in one day and night.

Favorite among the Laya Yogis is the mantra *"Om, aim, klim, strim."* "Om" is introductory; the other three are called "seed" mantras; *aim* being the seed of speech or intelligence, in the first lotus, *klim* the seed mantra of love, in the heart lotus, and *strim* the seed mantra of power, in the eyebrow lotus. On the *chitrini* canal at these points there are *granthis,* or "knots," which obstruct the advance of Kundalini. With the aid of these mantras they are broken through. Great results are said to accrue from many repetitions of this mantra, which must be said neither too quickly nor too slowly. At the lower end of the scale he who repeats it a hundred thousand times becomes "very attractive," and at the higher end, by ten million repetitions, the great yogi reaches the highest goal.

The mantra *Om,* which is used at the beginning and end of all prayers, needs special mention. It is considered to have a harmonizing effect, as being the word, or true name, not merely the appellative name, of the "one life without a second." It is composed of the three letters a, u, and m, and can be pronounced with the a and u both distinctly heard, or, as is more usual, with the two bunched together as *Om.* The meaning may be derived in the following way. As "a" is sounded from the throat, it is the beginning of all sounds, and as "m" is formed by the closing of the lips, it is the end, "u" being in the middle. Therefore when *Om* is properly sounded with a glide from one letter to the next, it is the complete word. And since sound is creative power, *Om* is not only the natural name of God, but pronunciation of it is a means to harmony with the divine.

The same idea is symbolically represented in the *Sandilya Upanishad,* where the yogi is told to meditate, using the *pranava,* that is, *Om,* at the same time thinking of three goddesses; Gayatri, a girl of reddish color, seated on a swan and carrying a mace, who represents the letter "a"; Savitri, a young woman of white color, mounted on an eagle and carrying a disc, who represents the letter "u"; and Saraswati, a mature woman of dark color, riding on a bull and carrying a trident, who represents the letter "m." These goddesses are the wives and *shaktis,* or powers, of the three members of the Trinity—Shiva, Vishnu and Brahma—who together constitute the one Brahman. (The yogi is told to use the proportions sixteen, sixty-four and thirty-two for breathing during this meditation.)

Generally, mantras have meanings, and must be recited with the mind intent upon them, but there are exceptions. So far as I am aware, *aim, klim* and *strim,* mentioned above, have none, but all the same they are to be recited with intention or purpose. In private recitation the low voice is considered to have much more effect than the loud.

Very closely allied psychologically with the Mantra Yoga is the practice of art in connection with religious matters. Just as the repetition of certain words helps the devotee to keep his mind well concentrated, so in the case of the temperament which runs to external creativeness, painting and sculpture is a means of holding up and preserving the desired emotional and mental states. The whole process is not very different from that of damming up a valley and so conserving the water for the constant use of the countryside. Art may very well be looked upon as a form of yoga. I have already referred to a passage in the *Bhagavad Gita* which says that yoga is skill in work. Skukracharya says: "Let the image-maker establish images in temples by meditation on the deities who are the objects of his devotion. In no other way, not even by direct and immediate vision of an actual object, is it possible to be so absorbed in contemplation as thus in the making of images."

Out of this inevitably comes beauty, even when the intention to do so is not intellectually formulated, for action well done always produces that effect in some natural way. Thus, for example, the limbs and figure of the race-horse are wonderfully beautiful, because of the skill developed in running, and also the running is beautiful to see. When an artist does his best, the same effect is produced, both in the man and in the work. This itself constitutes a kind of union with the divine, for if it can be said that God is expressible in material form, it must be in beauty, since that is the one thing in the material world of which the soul never tires.

Before closing this chapter on Hatha Yoga I must say that none of the standard works on the subject countenance physical mortification, such as withering the arm or sitting on spikes, but all aim at a good condition of bodily health, and in food, not fasting, but moderation. The examples of mortification occasionally seen may be regarded as cases of partial insanity, due generally to that fear of the future which, as Sir Edwin Arnold puts it in *The Light of Asia*, causes men to try to "baulk hell by self-kindled hells." So these practices of asceticism are not countenanced by any school of yoga.

As this subject is very important, I will indulge in a quotation on the subject from the *Garuda Purana*: "Donkeys walk about among people, in forests and among houses, quite naked and unashamed. Are these free from attachment? If men are to be liberated by earth, ashes and dust, does the dog which always lives among earth and ashes become liberated? Jackals, rats, deer, and others, which feed upon grass, leaves and water, and always live in forests—do these become ascetics? The crocodiles, fishes and others, which from birth to death dwell in the waters of Ganges—do these become Yogis? Pigeons at times eat stones, and Chataka birds do not drink water from the earth—are these observers of vows?"*

Similar verses occur in many other works. In the *Bhagavad Gita* Shri Krishna denounces those who practice mortification, which he calls horrible, and says that they are full of vanity, egotism and passion. "Being unintelligent, they torment the elements of the body, and me also within the body. Know them to be ungodly in their resolves."†

---

* *Garuda Purana Saroddhara,* xvi. 65-70.
† *Op. cit.,* xvii. 5, 6.

CHAPTER 6

PRACTICAL CONCENTRATION AND MEDITATION

There can be little doubt that most of those who read this book will be actuated not so much by a mere academic desire to know what are the psychological practices of the Hindus as by a wish to discover a means to awaken the undeveloped capacities of their own minds, and also in many cases to direct them to a goal worthwhile—something better than the squirrel cage of ordinary unambitious human existence.

In India an intelligent serenity has long been the ideal of practical life, and one does notice more calm strong faces, and eyes which appear to see the eternal, than in other countries—faces out of which the fever and hunger have gone, and which seem instead to reflect a quiet rippling of the heart. The two things which can produce such a peace are the discovery of the infinite in the finite, and a mind which has no foibles, clean or unclean. The interest in life of one who by thought in league with experience has won this goal is not in personal ambitions, bodily sensations, or mental foibles, but in life itself in all its forms. It is natural for us to love, when personal fear, greed and pride do not get in the way. That is why all like flowers and young things, even the tiger cub. Really all people are flowers and tigers.

The opportunity for this universality, or the finding of the infinite in the finite, is ever present. We may quite naturally love even our enemies when the mind is no longer lashed into a storm of unnatural and undignified sensations and emotions. It is sufficient to see the supreme in one thing in order afterwards to see it everywhere. To learn the piano I need one instrument, not a million. If I have loved one mother, I can love all mothers. One friend introduces me to all people. I will not try to sing the praises of love, as I would not talk of colors to a blind man. If it is known, it is known. But I would say seek it, because love and thought, and that dignity which is the will, are the open doorways to eternal life, which no circumstances can ever be.

I almost doubt the value of training the mind, when I see the superlative power of even the smallest vision of the eternal, and that life is not quiescent, but a bubbling, dancing, happy thing. I cannot say that life is fond of work, but I do see that when not clouded by dull care, which is always unnecessary, it plays, and there is no use in questioning this. I see, too, that the play of life, true to itself, and when not losing its nature of intelligence and love, is more fruitful than that stupidity called work.

I am offering some hints about the training of the mind, as a fitting conclusion to this study of occult training. But I would suggest as the greatest secret of success in this matter that all its undertakings should be done in a spirit of play, not of work.

Concentration

Concentration is the narrowing of the field of attention in a manner and for a time determined by the will. Our consciousness may at any given time be diffused over a large area, in which everything is indefinite, or it may be focused on some chosen object. In the latter case, we obtain the clearest mental vision and the most vivid consciousness of which we are capable. The practice of concentration is intended to produce this condition, and may be carried out with the aid of the following hints:

1. Go into a room by yourself, sit down, close your eyes, and observe what happens when you think about an elephant. You will soon see that two mental processes are going on. The first is that the idea of the elephant seems to be a kind of box, containing many other ideas, and as you concentrate upon it these ideas come forth and stand round it. You may see there special pictures of particular parts of the elephant, such as its large ear or its peculiar trunk; you may think of its intelligence and philosophical temperament, or of elephants that you have seen. These ideas arise not by accident, but according to definite laws, for there are roads which the human mind has made through the jungle of the thought world, just as men have made roads in the outer world. So, when you think of an elephant, you may also think of a hippopotamus or a rhinoceros, or ivory, or the zoological gardens or India—you are not likely to think of a humming-bird or a silk hat. In the mental world there are laws analogous to those

of gravitation, magnetism, cohesion and the like in the physical world.

I have explained the "roads of thought" fully in my book *Memory Training*, but will here summarize them in four groups. The first law of idea attraction is that thoughts of similar things cling closely together and suggest one another. We may call it the road of Object and Class, and Objects of the same Class. The second law connects Whole and Part; for example, thinking of the elephant, ideas of its tail and ears and trunk would come up—you are not likely to think of the sails of a ship or the carburetor of a motor car engine. The third law expresses the relation between Object and Quality; thus one thinks of the elephant's weight and sagacity, or of the devotion of a dog, or the artistic tendencies of a cat. The fourth law may be entitled Familiar Experience. Thus, for example, if I think of a pen, I shall probably think also of ink, not of whitewash; or if I think of a bed, I shall think of sleep, not of dancing. All the connections of what are usually called cause and effect also come within this law, as, for example, in the relation of sunrise and daylight.

The second process is often called mind-wandering, though it is really very indefinite thinking. If you try to concentrate on an elephant for a few minutes, you may very soon find yourself thinking about something totally different, having forgotten the elephant altogether. Still, your attention has not jumped. You have thought perhaps first of the elephant, then of the timber yards of Rangoon, then of the woodwork in the new house that you are building, then of delay in the building, and now you suddenly wake up to find yourself worrying over that. There has been a definite passage from one thought to another. If you can control that chain of thought, and compel it to follow a definite line, just as you control your legs and make them go along a predetermined road whenever you take a walk, you will be really thinking. This involves some effort, because it is somewhat like going uphill; but the drift of thought in mind-wandering is like that of water finding its way downhill, at each movement taking the easiest or most familiar path.

2. Select a subject and settle down to concentrate upon it for five minutes. Some people sit down and shut their eyes, and then begin to try to decide what they will concentrate upon, and after changing their minds several times, because they do not quite like the subject that they have thus casually chosen, they find their time already gone. But you should first select your subject—some common object, such as an orange, then sit down and say to yourself: "Now I am going to keep my mental eye on that orange for five minutes, without losing sight of it, and I am not interested in anything else during that time. There is plenty of time outside this five minutes for other things." Then close your eyes, and begin. You should not give yourself an indefinite time for this practice. Give yourself five minutes exactly. If you are hungry for more, give yourself another five minutes, but at least three hours later. It does not

matter if you are unable to visualize the orange, as long as you can keep it in the mind's eye.

3. Do not try to *hold* the object before your mental vision. The aim of concentration is not to grasp the chosen object, but to stop the mind from wandering away from it. Look at it perfectly quietly and calmly, just as you would look at anything normally with your physical eye. There is no need to stare with great fixity at your watch, in order to see the time. Look with similar calmness at the orange. In the beginning imagine that the orange is lying on a plate on the table. When you first close your eyes, you will thus imagine it there, and the whole room will be in your thought to some extent. Let your mind dwell on the entire room for a moment, and then narrow down the field of attention to the table, the plate, and finally the orange. You will then have no sense of holding up the orange. You ought also to have absolutely no tension in the body, or anywhere in the head. To crease the brow, and clench the jaws and fists, and tense the muscles of the neck and swell the blood-vessels is not mental concentration. The yogis say that the brow of the great thinker is smooth and calm; it is the very reverse of what is depicted in Rodin's famous statue of "The Thinker." That shows the man who is trying to think, and does not know how to do it.

4. The mind and the physical body being thus quite calm, you have next to consider the emotions. These are a prolific source of interruption in concentration. Though people do not usually notice it, the

mind is full of little disturbances, which easily arise during concentration, so that quite often you may find yourself troubled by what somebody said yesterday, or what is likely to happen tomorrow. It is possible, by an effort of the will, to cast those thoughts out whenever they appear, but that is not the best way to deal with them. It is better to quieten the emotional nature by applying the formula, "I don't care." As soon as one of the intruders catches the mental eye, you say, "Hello, are *you* there? Well, I don't care. Stay if you like; go if you like. I am busy, looking at this orange and cannot attend to you." It will then quietly fade out; but you cannot have the satisfaction of watching it do so, just as you cannot see yourself go to sleep. Do not trouble yourself if other things come vaguely into the neighborhood of your chosen thought, provided that that remains in the center of the stage. There is no boundary to a thought-picture. You do not draw a line and keep within that, but your picture shades off gradually from the central object that you have chosen, and all you have to do is to see that you keep your eye on that center.

5. During the five minutes, practice recall by the method described in my book on *Concentration*, which is briefly as follows: Having settled your attention upon the chosen object, think of all that you can about it without going away from it. In this practice it is best to follow the four roads of thought. First think of the class of things to which the orange belongs, that is, edible fruit, and of other members of

the same class. Then think of its parts, and of the greater whole of which it is a part, that is to say, the tree. Then think of its qualities for each of the senses, its shape, color, weight, etc. And finally think of oranges you have known, and other thoughts familiarly associated with the subject, such as Spain and California and marmalade.

By this means you will have set up a habit of the mind to keep its attention to one thing until you have brought out all your possible thoughts in connection with it. You will have arranged all your knowledge on the subject. You will know what an orange is as you never did before, and your mind will be awake to it and interested in it—just as a man who has newly and for the first time acquired a motor car has a keen eye for every one on the road. This practice, which after some time may be permitted to continue for fifteen minutes at a sitting, should be applied at first to common objects, but later on it may equally well be applied to difficult and abstract subjects.

As a result of these practices, concentration will suddenly become easy. It is something like swimming. Many times, perhaps, you have entered the water, and clutching it fiercely with hand and mouth, you have sunk beneath it again and again, but one day you found yourself at home in the water, and then you could swim and float. And after that, always before entering the water, you almost unconsciously put on a certain mood of the mind, which acts on the body so that it assumes the right condition and position for swimming. So it is with concentration. Having achieved it once, you become aware of a certain mood which makes it quite easy thereafter. Then you will find that concentration is a power, and that its application to a thought even for a moment can do wonders in impressing it upon the memory, or in opening up its possibilities.

Meditation

At any given time, meditation is to be practiced only after concentration. Some people try to jump, as it were, straight into meditation, but in doing so they fail to achieve the vividness of vision that concentration gives. Meditation is expansion, where concentration is contraction. By concentration you have reached your best state of consciousness; in meditation you must keep that state of consciousness, but enlarge its field. Meditation in which the concentration lapses is a failure. In concentration, also, one usually begins on a material or simple thing; but in meditation one carries the clear conception of that simple thing to levels of thought more abstract or complex and difficult to hold. There are thus two consequences to meditation; you enlarge your scope and you develop your power. It is thus real thinking, and a creative exercise.

To make this clear, imagine a tall jar, and let us suppose that it is marked with horizontal lines into divisions, and someone is pouring water into that jar from above. Now, if there are a great many little holes all round the bottom and sides of the jar, the water will run out, and the level in the jar may not rise very high; but if the holes are filled up the water rises. Most people are like jars full of holes, always ready to leak all over the place, being quite uncontrolled. But concentration, starting with its quietness of the physical body, and then of the emotions, and then of the mind, stops up all the holes.

Meditation is the flow of the water from above, and as long as it is clear and strong, plenty of water is coming down and filling up the vessel quite steadily. Thus by meditation you observe the object in detail and accurately, and you proceed to understand its functions in relation to other things.

Meditation is thus the opposite of going to sleep. In it you make the body quiet, but keep the mind alert, and carry up to higher and broader conditions of thought the clearness of consciousness that you have acquired by concentration.

Meditation may be practiced with the aid of the following hints:

1. Sit down as before, and concentrate on a cat, bringing the subject fully forward by means of the four roads of thought. Then think of the cat in a wider significance, making your lines of thought go further than they did before, but still without losing sight of the cat. It is just as though, in the example of the elephant, you could think of the timber yards, of your new house, of the delay, and even more, without losing sight of the elephant. This is the expansive meditation. It is not essentially different from thinking, but it does not go out of sight of a

chosen center. Thus a student of geometry, in the working out of a proposition, has certain data before him. He should first concentrate on the data, and then start his flow of thought, and then go as far as possible in the direction of his solution without losing sight of his data, and what they involve. When he loses sight of those, his thread breaks and he has to begin again.

2. Once more take the cat as subject, and carry your thought inward and upward. Dwell first on the physical nature of your cat, then try to realize what its emotions are, then if possible its mental nature, and even its moral and spiritual condition, if such can be discerned. This method may be applied also to meditations on the virtues, which have a prominent place in yoga and in religious practices generally. A person selects a quality such as kindness or courage, and generally begins to dwell upon it without realizing that he has a most inadequate conception as to what it really is. Ask a person what kind of figures are on the dial of his watch, and very often he cannot tell you rightly, though he may have had it for years. Or ask him the difference between running and walking—two acts which most people think themselves able to imagine as well as to perform. It will probably be some time before he realizes that in running both feet are off the ground at the same time, but in walking one is always touching it. If people have such imperfect ideas about common things like that, what must be said with regard to their conceptions of kindness and courage? Medita-

tion on these virtues should be so arranged as to
create a clear realization of what they are, and then
build them into the character.

First of all, then, make some pictures of concrete
acts of kindness or courage. Make a picture of a
soldier bringing in a wounded comrade under fire,
an invalid taking his lesson in the right spirit, a
young artist keeping to his purpose in the face of
great discouragement, or one pursuing with cheerfulness a disagreeable task that is a duty. These pictures may or may not be clearly visualized. Many
persons have a species of tactual visualization, if so it
may be called, by means of which the idea is perfectly
clear in detail, they are in conscious touch with it,
and yet it would not be quite accurate to say that
they see it. It will take some time to make each picture, and a number of sittings are necessary to make
a little collection of them on one topic. When, however, one has been made and concentrated upon, it
will reappear with great alacrity when called up by
the will in subsequent sittings. Make these pictures
solid and living, like a drama played upon a stage,
not flat, like a picture on a wall.

When the pictures are ready, go over them in
meditation, trying to realize the state of feeling and
emotion and afterwards the state of mind of the char-
acters in them, and again with a view to grasping
the abstract idea of the virtue. Finally, in order to
build this courage into your own character, go over
the pictures again, but this time step up onto the
stage and take the place of the hero depicted there,

and feel yourself acting the part. Thus one may practice a little each day for about a month on one virtue.

3. Sometimes a devotee wants to meditate on the
ideal man, with a definite face before him, but finds
it difficult to hold the complete thing in imagination.
In that case he may build it up in the following manner. First of all concentrate on one portion, such as
an eye; then drop that and concentrate on another
portion, say the other eye. Then recall the first and
make a joint picture of the two. Drop that and concentrate on a third portion, say the nose. Then recall
the other pair and make a joint picture of the three,
and so on. Thus he will have given equal attention
and full concentration to forming each portion, and
in the end the whole picture will be equally clear in
every part. In India, not so much attention would
usually be given to the physical features, as to the
form, containing a great variety of symbolical detail,
and suggesting many trains of thought, as in the following example, translated by Pandit Rama Prasada,
from one of the Puranas:

> The personified appearance of the Lord leaves no
> room for the desire to possess any other object of
> concentration. The fact of the mind being held fast
> there is what is called concentration. And, O King,
> hear what that personified appearance of the Lord
> is that should be meditated upon; there can be no
> concentration without something upon which the
> mind may rest. The face is cheerful and pleasing to
> the mind, the eyes are full of freshness and depth
> like lotus leaves, the cheeks are beautiful, the
> forehead is bright and high, the ears are sym-

metrical and well adorned by drops, the neck is long like the shell of a conch; the auspicious sign of fortune, a curl of white hair, appears on his breast; with a deep navel and deep furrows appearing in the abdomen; with eight or four arms hanging from his body; sitting with thighs and shanks evenly placed, and hands and feet placed in the form of a Svastika. Such is the appearance of Vishnu, clad in clean yellow garb, adorned with beautiful head-dress, armlet, bracelet, etc.; carrying his bow, his discus, his club, his sword, his conch shell and his rosary of Rudraksha. He has become Brahma. With mind merged in him, let the yogi devote himself to meditating upon him. Let him apply his mind to him so long as his concentration becomes well established. Practicing this concentration or doing some other work in accordance with his own wishes, so long as the mind learns not to get away from the object of concentration, the yogi should in that state consider his concentration achieved.

4. There are two other general practices which should be undertaken by all who wish to make a success of formal, scientific meditation. One of these was spoken of in a general way by Emerson as "reading for correction." The practice is to think first and read afterwards. Every aspirant should always have a good book on hand, on some subject that requires thought, and several times a week, when he can give half an hour or more to it, he should quietly proceed to read it, on each occasion thinking first for about ten minutes of what he is going to read about, and then giving about twenty minutes to the reading. In this case the mind brings forth in review what it

knows on the subject, however little, and also a number of questions, some of them quite unformulated. Thus a kind of mental mold is made, in which the new knowledge will take its place, and many mental grappling irons are ready to take hold of the author's information and meaning.

The second practice consists of quiet reflection in the evening upon the occurrences of the day, or in the morning in anticipation of the day's work. This meditation is not formal—one just turns things over and looks at them very quietly—but it is nevertheless a source of much inspiration.

Contemplation

Contemplation may be briefly described as another form of concentration, in which one's attention is fixed upon the highest aspect of the subject that one can reach. It is the third step in the series. Meditation should not be dropped suddenly, just as it should not be begun suddenly, but when you have reached the highest point that you can without loss of strength, or when you have a flash of illumination, do not try to go forward, and do not turn back, but concentrate upon that for at least a few moments. Contemplation is concentration at the top end of your line of thought. Thus a new platform is produced in the mind. This applies to scientific thinking and secular matters just as much as to philosophic and religious studies and purposes.

This state is sometimes reached involuntarily by devotees in whom a chosen image or picture, or the sight perhaps of some glorious natural beauty, awakens an ecstatic feeling, and they stand transfixed, drinking in, in complete self-forgetfulness, the beautiful realities. This is worship, the highest human faculty, in which man contacts truth, goodness and beauty beyond the limited personally relative experiences and conceptions of them which are already familiar to him.

Occultism

Contemplation, deliberately practiced with regard to an object, opens up the avenues of intuitional knowledge connected with it, and thus also the way to many of the powers that people think of as occultism. It is true that these powers are occult as being hidden from the ordinary man, but to the yogi they are in no way marvelous. They are nothing more than an extension of those which are used every day by all people, and are not therefore really the hidden powers. But the aim of the true occultist is not merely to enlarge the world of his experience in that manner, with new powers and the new problems that they bring.

Occultism may be defined as the use of the hidden powers in man to discover the hidden life in the world. It has thus rightly been said that it is *atma-vidya,* the science of the Self, and that its object is to discover the Divine Mind in nature. Through the faculties and powers of the personality a man comes in contact with phenomena, and learns through them, as a child with toys. But with the powers of the higher Self—its will, and love and thought, working in outward things, but unshaken by them, and not confused by personality—a man may penetrate through the veil of appearances, and the hidden reality in him will deal with the hidden reality behind phenomena. This man works through intuition—no longer a child, he deals with realities, not with toys. Such is the occultist, and to such a goal is directed the occult training of the Hindus.

THE THEOSOPHICAL PUBLISHING HOUSE

Wheaton, Ill., U.S.A.

Madras, India   London, England

Publishers of a wide range of titles on many
subjects including:

> *Mysticism*
>
> *Yoga*
>
> *Meditation*
>
> *Extrasensory Perception*
>
> *Religions of the World*
>
> *Asian Classics*
>
> *Reincarnation*
>
> *The Human Situation*
>
> *Theosophy*

Distributors for the Adyar Library Series of Sanskrit
Texts, Translations and Studies

The Theosophical Publishing House, Wheaton,
Illinois, is also the publisher of

QUEST BOOKS

Many titles from our regular clothbound list in
attractive paperbound editions

*For a complete descriptive list of all Quest Books
write to:*

QUEST BOOKS
P.O. Box 270, Wheaton, Ill. 60187